ORACLE

The Divine
Communication

ORACLE

The Divine Communication

Vinu V Das

Tabor Press

ISBN: 978-1-997541-11-0

Table of Contents

Chapter 1: The Voice of God – Understanding the Oracle

The Word of God holds a preeminent place in Christian belief as the foundation for faith and practice. Throughout biblical history, God has spoken in various ways: through a booming voice from heaven, through dreams that stirred the hearts of rulers and commoners alike, through subtle nudges that directed the course of events, and at times through the still small voice heard by prophets and ordinary believers. An "oracle" in a biblical sense encompasses all forms of I— messages that originate with God and are revealed to human beings in order to convey truth, direction, admonition, or comfort.

An oracle is more than mere prophecy—it is the articulation of divine wisdom, sometimes delivered through a prophet but just as often encountered in private communication between God and an individual. By studying these foundational ideas, we begin to understand how the divine voice not only shapes biblical narratives but also informs Christian thought and spiritual practice today.

1.1 Defining the Oracle in Scripture

1.1.1 Etymology and Usage of Hebrew and Greek Terms

The English word "oracle" often conjures images of mysterious voices echoing from ancient shrines, but the biblical concept is both broader and deeper. In Hebrew, one frequently encountered root associated with divine utterance is נְאֻם (ne'um), often translated as "declares" or "oracle" in the Old Testament. This term appears in phrases such as "declares the LORD" to underscore that what follows is not merely human wisdom but a direct articulation from God. When biblical writers employ this word, they intend to stress the divine authority behind the message. Another Hebrew term, often rendered "burden" or "pronouncement," is מַשָּׂא (massa'), which can be linked to prophetic "oracles" that contain warnings or judgments.

In the Greek New Testament, the concepts of *logos* (λόγος) and *rhema* (ῥῆμα) stand out. While both can be translated as "word," *logos* often carries the sense of reasoned discourse or the broader content of God's message, whereas *rhema* points more specifically to the spoken word or the utterance in a precise moment. The distinction is not always rigid, but it can help in understanding the multifaceted ways the New Testament writers perceived God's self-revelation. In Romans 3:2, for example, Paul refers to the "oracles of God" entrusted to the Jewish people, highlighting the divine instructions, commands, and revelations that were given uniquely to Israel.

1.1.2 Old Testament Foundations of the Oracle Concept

From the earliest chapters of Genesis, we see God speaking creation into existence with His word (Genesis 1:3, "And God said…"). This creative speech sets the tone for the entire biblical narrative: whenever God speaks, something happens. When He spoke to Adam, it was in the context of providing instructions and establishing relationship (Genesis 2:16–17). This pattern continues throughout the Old Testament, as God reveals Himself to individuals and communities through direct communication—sometimes audibly, sometimes through intermediaries, and sometimes in dramatic, miraculous ways.

Crucial to the Old Testament understanding of the oracle is the notion that when God speaks, His words carry inherent authority and power. In Isaiah 55:11, we read that His word "shall not return…void, but it shall accomplish that which [He] purposes." This demonstrates the belief that the divine utterance is performative; it does not merely state facts but enacts the will of God in the created order. Whether these words are directives to His people or declarations about future events, they are fully reliable as they originate from the One who is altogether truthful and sovereign.

Moreover, the oracle is not confined to any single mode of communication. It may come as a warning—such as God's word to Cain in Genesis 4:6–7, urging him to master sin before it overtakes him—or a promise, as in Genesis 12:1–3, when the Lord calls Abraham to leave his homeland, assuring him of blessing. These diverse forms of divine utterance form the backdrop for understanding how central the oracle is in shaping the faith and identity of God's people throughout the Old Testament era.

1.1.3 The Sacredness and Authority of the Oracle

Because the oracle is believed to stem from the mouth of God, it carries ultimate authority. Human beings who disregard or fail to heed the oracle do so at their own peril. The repeated biblical refrain, "Thus says the Lord," underscores that the speaker—whether a prophet, a king, or a writer of Scripture—is not the originator of the message but merely the vessel through which the divine Word is delivered. In passages like Jeremiah 1:9–10, we see God touching Jeremiah's mouth and commissioning him to speak whatever God commands. The words Jeremiah proclaimed were not his own invention; they were "the words of the LORD."

The emphasis on divine authority also explains why the Old Testament is filled with references to blessings for obedience to God's word and curses for disobedience. When Moses communicated God's commands to Israel, he repeatedly warned them to listen carefully to God's voice (Deuteronomy 28). The stakes were not limited to personal moral failing; entire communities and even future generations could be affected by how they responded to the divine Word. Consequently, the concept of the oracle, or the Word of God, was always deeply interwoven with covenant blessings and curses.

1.1.4 The Continuum of Proclamation and Silence

One fascinating aspect of the biblical narrative is the alternating pattern of divine proclamation and periods of apparent silence. At times, God's voice rings loud and clear: storms parted, seas parted, and nations trembled. Yet Scripture also records periods when "the word of the Lord was rare," as in 1 Samuel 3:1. Such intervals highlight both the preciousness of divine revelation and the responsibility placed upon those who receive it. When God does speak, the message is urgent, transformative, and calls for a response.

The interplay between silence and speech underscores the seriousness with which biblical people approached the oracle. If the Word of the Lord was not always constant, then those who were privileged to receive it recognized the need to hear and obey carefully. This dynamic tension further enriches the Old Testament understanding of the oracle, setting the stage for how the faithful awaited every word that proceeded from God's mouth (Deuteronomy 8:3).

1.1.5 Distinguishing Between True and False Oracles

While it is primarily in other parts of Scripture (especially the prophetic books) that the distinction between true and false prophecy is fleshed out, a foundational principle emerges in the Old Testament: a true oracle aligns with God's character and covenantal promises. Deuteronomy 13:1–5 warns the Israelites against any prophet who might lead them away from the worship of the true God, even if that prophet's signs and wonders appear convincing. Thus, authenticity is not merely about miraculous demonstration but hinges on fidelity to God's revealed nature and commands.

This underscores that the concept of the oracle is not a casual phenomenon but a sacred trust. Since God Himself is holy, consistent, and truthful, any genuine oracle bearing His signature must reflect that holiness, consistency, and truthfulness. This belief established a stringent criterion by which oracles could be tested and validated, further emphasizing their divine origin and unassailable authority when they were indeed genuine.

1.2 The Oracle as Divine Communication

1.2.1 The Multiform Ways God Speaks

Scripture records a variety of ways in which God communicates, reflecting His desire to relate to humanity in contexts they can understand. One of the first explicit episodes of God's voice in Scripture is found in Genesis 3:9, where the Lord calls out to Adam and Eve in the garden. Here, the communication is direct and personal. Throughout the Old Testament, some of the most notable "oracular moments" involve God meeting His people where they are—whether that is in a burning bush (Exodus 3:4), a gentle whisper on a mountainside (1 Kings 19:12–13), or thunderous proclamations from the heavens (Exodus 19:18–19).

Dreams and Visions: Many biblical figures, such as Joseph (Genesis 37) or Daniel (Daniel 2 and 4), received divine revelation through dreams. These dreams often contained symbolism that required interpretation, reinforcing the idea that God's voice can come in unexpected ways. Visions, though closely related to dreams, typically occur when the recipient is awake. For example, Ezekiel experienced a series of dramatic visions (Ezekiel 1) that conveyed God's glory and directed him to communicate specific messages.

Audible and Direct Speech: At times, God's communication in Scripture is portrayed as an audible voice. Moses stands as a prime example—he frequently conversed with God, especially during the wilderness period, as illustrated in Exodus 33:11, which describes the Lord speaking to Moses "face to face." Such direct interaction underscores a profound closeness between God and the one receiving the message, though this closeness is often coupled with reverence and even fear.

1.2.2 The Purpose Behind God's Communication

Each instance of divine communication in the Bible comes with intent. God does not speak arbitrarily; He speaks to convey His character and to align His people with His will. This may include revealing plans for the future, disclosing truths about the present, issuing corrections, offering comfort, or reaffirming covenant promises.

1. **Revelation of Identity and Character:** In Exodus 3:14, when Moses inquires about God's name, God replies, "I AM WHO I AM," revealing something of His eternal, self-existent nature. This fundamental disclosure serves as more than mere information—it is a transformative revelation that shapes Moses' understanding of who God is and how Moses should serve Him.
2. **Guidance and Instruction:** Many biblical oracles provide direction. The instructions given to Noah for building the ark (Genesis 6) or to Joshua on how to conquer Jericho (Joshua 6) show that when God speaks, He not only commands but also provides the strategy, timing, and moral framework for action.
3. **Warning and Correction:** In several instances, particularly in the Old Testament, God's words come as stark warnings to individuals or nations. Even in such "negative" oracles, the heart of God's message often points to repentance and restoration. For example, God warned Cain in Genesis 4:7 that sin was crouching at his door, urging him to rule over it rather than succumb to it.
4. **Encouragement and Comfort:** In times of distress or need, God's voice brings comfort. Passages like Psalm 46:10 ("Be still, and know that I am God") offer

an oracular reassurance of God's sovereignty and nearness, even amidst chaos and fear.

1.2.3 Symbolic and Theophanic Dimensions

A profound aspect of divine communication is the presence of symbols, metaphors, and theophanies (manifestations of God's presence). Sometimes the revelation does not come through straightforward speech but through a tangible sign or physical phenomenon. The pillar of cloud and fire that led the Israelites through the wilderness (Exodus 13:21–22) functioned as an ongoing, visible manifestation of God's guidance—an "oracle in motion," so to speak.

Symbolism in dreams, as in Joseph's sheaves of wheat or Daniel's visions of beasts, stands as another layer of God's communication. These symbolic representations often serve a dual purpose: they partially veil the message to ensure its timely and appropriate unveiling, and they captivate the recipient's attention to engage deeply with its meaning. Such forms of communication demand spiritual discernment, inviting recipients to seek God more earnestly for wisdom and clarity (Daniel 2:20–23).

1.2.4 The Dynamic of Ongoing Dialogue

A notable pattern in Scripture is that God's communication is not typically a one-off event; rather, it often unfolds as part of a sustained relationship or dialogue. This is evident in the lives of figures like Abraham, who conversed repeatedly with God about the future of his descendants (Genesis 15, 17, 18). The repeated dialogues suggest that God's oracles are relational, meant to develop trust, obedience, and a deeper understanding of divine purpose.

From a biblical perspective, the divine-human relationship can grow only if there is true communion—an exchange of revelation from God and an earnest seeking from humanity. This synergy is not about humans merely receiving instructions but about them learning to recognize God's voice. Over time, figures like Samuel (1 Samuel 3) and David (1

Samuel 23:2) demonstrate increased sensitivity to God's prompting, highlighting that discerning God's voice becomes more refined through practice, humility, and obedience.

1.2.5 Boundaries and Limits on Human Comprehension

Although God communicates out of a desire to be known, Scripture also teaches that He remains transcendent. This paradox means that while God's oracle is accessible and understandable at a certain level, it also exceeds full human comprehension. Deuteronomy 29:29 underscores that "the secret things belong to the Lord," reminding readers that not all knowledge or divine reasoning will be disclosed. Consequently, the biblical narrative often depicts individuals wrestling with the meaning of an oracle, uncertain of its timing, or initially misunderstanding its scope.

This inherent limitation should not discourage believers but rather cultivate humility and awe. When Daniel received visions, he was sometimes left distressed (Daniel 7:15, 7:28), reflecting the burden of glimpsing divine mysteries. Such experiences highlight that God's ways and thoughts are higher than ours (Isaiah 55:9). Therefore, even when God speaks, He does so in a manner that sustains reverence for His holiness and majesty, encouraging humanity to trust and obey rather than fully grasp every detail at once.

1.3 Human Response to God's Voice

1.3.1 Fear as a Natural Response

A frequent reaction to divine communication in the Bible is fear or awe, sometimes accompanied by trembling or a sense of unworthiness. When God descended on Mount Sinai in a visible display of power—thunder, lightning, and the sound of a trumpet—the Israelites were terrified and requested that Moses speak to God on their behalf (Exodus 20:18–19). This response arises from the sudden realization that the voice speaking is not a mere earthly authority but the One who created the cosmos and sustains all life.

Fear, in this sense, is not always negative; Scripture often frames it as a "holy fear" or reverent awe. Proverbs 9:10 calls the fear of the Lord "the beginning of wisdom," implying that recognizing God's unmatched power and holiness is the gateway to true understanding. This reverence can propel individuals toward deeper devotion and a desire to remain in right standing with God.

At the same time, the Bible also records instances where fear becomes debilitating—leading people to shrink back rather than drawing near to God. Gideon's initial reaction in Judges 6:22–23 demonstrates a mix of awe and apprehension, as he fears he might die after encountering the "angel of the Lord." Yet God reassures him with peace, an invitation to rely on divine guidance rather than be paralyzed by dread.

1.3.2 Obedience and Willing Surrender

In many biblical accounts, the oracle of God prompts transformative obedience. Abraham's story stands as one of the most striking examples: when God speaks to him in Genesis 12, instructing him to leave his homeland, Abraham responds in faith. This obedience sets in motion the entire narrative of God's covenant people. Even though Abraham did not know exactly where he was going, his trust in the divine word established a pattern of faithful surrender for generations to come.

Similarly, figures like Noah (Genesis 6) and Joshua (Joshua 1) demonstrate how obedience to God's voice brings about both personal and communal blessings. This alignment with God's will is not always easy; it often involves personal sacrifice, confronting opposition, or venturing into uncharted territory. Yet the biblical witness consistently affirms that such obedience to the oracle is life-giving and ultimately rewarding (Deuteronomy 28:1–2).

1.3.3 Resistance and Doubt

Not all who hear God's voice respond positively. Accounts of resistance to divine communication appear throughout

Scripture, showcasing the tension between human free will and divine sovereignty. A prime example is Pharaoh's hardened heart in the Exodus narrative. Despite Moses repeatedly conveying God's command to let the Israelites go, Pharaoh persists in stubborn rebellion (Exodus 5–14). His refusal to heed the oracle leads to devastating plagues and, ultimately, the loss of his army in the Red Sea.

On a personal level, even individuals who yearn for God's direction might struggle with doubt or incredulity. Sarah, upon overhearing the divine promise that she would bear a son in her old age, laughed to herself (Genesis 18:12), indicating disbelief at the seeming impossibility of God's word. Though in time she recognized the miracle as God's work, her initial skepticism is a vivid portrayal of the human tendency to question the feasibility of divine pronouncements.

In certain cases, those who resist or doubt God's oracle do so because the message confronts their pride, challenges their preconceived notions, or requires them to relinquish control. Jonah famously fled in the opposite direction after receiving God's instruction to go to Nineveh (Jonah 1:1–3). His story underscores that even those called to carry the oracle of the Lord can resist it if it clashes with their personal preferences or prejudices.

1.3.4 The Growth Process in Responding to the Oracle

Recognizing that human responses range from fear to obedience to outright defiance, Scripture also illustrates that people can grow in their ability to discern and respond positively to God's voice over time. Samuel's early experience in 1 Samuel 3 is a classic example: as a boy ministering under Eli the priest, Samuel hears someone calling his name. Unaware that it is the Lord, he initially runs to Eli. Only after Eli instructs him to say, "Speak, Lord, for your servant hears" does Samuel begin to engage directly with God's voice.

This process-oriented perspective reminds believers that learning to hear and obey God is not typically a one-time event but an ongoing spiritual discipline. The repeated testing of faith, the practice of prayer, meditation on Scripture, and waiting upon the Lord can sharpen one's spiritual ears. Over time, this leads to greater clarity in discerning what is truly of God and fosters a more immediate willingness to obey.

1.3.5 Consequences of Obedience and Disobedience

The Bible is replete with examples illustrating that how one responds to God's oracle has tangible consequences. For those who obey, blessings often follow, though these blessings are not always material or immediate. They can include deeper fellowship with God, spiritual growth, and the fulfilling of God's purposes in and through one's life. In contrast, disobedience can lead to spiritual barrenness, personal or communal suffering, and missed opportunities to participate in God's redemptive work.

This principle is vividly depicted in narratives such as Saul's partial obedience in 1 Samuel 15. Saul was instructed to destroy the Amalekites completely but chose to spare their king and the best of their livestock. This disobedience, though seemingly minor from a human viewpoint, cost him his kingship because he failed to adhere to the Word of the Lord. The interplay between divine oracle and human responsibility is thus a defining aspect of the biblical faith, underscoring that every response carries significance.

Chapter 2: The Prophetic Office – Vessels of the Oracle

In the biblical narrative, few roles carry as much spiritual gravity and significance as that of the prophet. Prophets are central to understanding how God chose to speak to His covenant people, especially throughout the Old Testament era. Far from simply foretelling the future, these individuals served as mouthpieces for divine truth—often confronting moral failings, guiding national decisions, and calling the people back to covenant fidelity. They bore both the privilege and the burden of declaring the "Word of the Lord" in circumstances where obedience was seldom easy and opposition was frequent.

Unlike the priests, whose primary function involved officiating religious rituals, and kings, who governed national affairs, the prophets stood in a space uniquely dedicated to receiving and delivering God's oracles. This chapter explores the multifaceted nature of this sacred office.

2.1 The Role of Prophets in the Old Testament

2.1.1 Historical and Cultural Background

The ancient Near East was a milieu of diverse religious practices and beliefs, and the figure of a prophet was not unique to Israel. Other cultures, such as the Babylonians, Egyptians, and Canaanites, had their own versions of diviners, seers, and spiritual mediators who sought to discern the will of their deities. What set Israelite prophets apart was their strict allegiance to Yahweh—the God who revealed Himself through covenants, commandments, and a distinct moral and ethical framework. Rather than simply reading omens or performing ecstatic rituals, Israel's prophets were called to speak on behalf of the one true God who transcends the created order.

In the earliest historical books of the Old Testament, we see glimpses of prophetic figures offering counsel to leaders. For instance, individuals like Deborah (Judges 4–5) are described as both judges and prophets, bridging the gap between governance and divine revelation. The rise of Samuel (1 Samuel 1–3) marks a transition point, as he becomes a "kingmaker," anointing Israel's first monarch (Saul) and later David. During this period, the role of the prophet evolved from sporadic leadership to an institution crucial for guiding the nation's moral and spiritual direction.

2.1.2 Moses as the Prototype

Although technically predating the established monarchy, Moses is often considered the archetypal prophet in the Old Testament. Deuteronomy 18:15 records Moses telling the Israelites, "The Lord your God will raise up for you a prophet like me from among you... you shall listen to him." This statement not only underscores Moses' extraordinary calling—delivering Israel from bondage in Egypt, mediating the Sinai Covenant, and instituting God's law—but also sets a benchmark against which future prophets might be measured.

Moses' experience exemplifies the multifaceted dimensions of prophetic ministry. He held intimate conversations with God, sometimes described as "face to face" encounters (Exodus 33:11). Moses was entrusted with the Ten Commandments (Exodus 20), which formed the foundation of Israel's covenantal identity. His role extended to teaching, interceding on behalf of the people, adjudicating disputes, and leading the nation through perilous circumstances. This combination of spiritual and administrative duties foreshadowed how many later prophets would speak not only to religious matters but also to political and social realities.

2.1.3 Major and Minor Prophets in the Hebrew Scriptures

The phrase "Major Prophets" generally refers to the longer Old Testament books attributed to prophets like Isaiah, Jeremiah, and Ezekiel, while "Minor Prophets" refers to the shorter books spanning Hosea through Malachi. The designation "major" or "minor" does not reflect their importance but rather the length and scope of their writings. These texts preserve a significant array of oracles that were spoken over centuries, addressing both immediate historical crises and long-range divine plans.

1. **Isaiah:** Ministered primarily in Jerusalem, speaking to the kings of Judah during times of threat from foreign empires like Assyria. His messages interwove judgment with promises of redemption, highlighting God's sovereignty over all nations (Isaiah 6, 7, 9, 53).
2. **Jeremiah:** Known as the "weeping prophet," Jeremiah served during the final days of the kingdom of Judah, warning of impending exile if the people persisted in idolatry. His oracles often carried intense emotional weight, as he struggled with the hardened hearts of his compatriots (Jeremiah 1, 20, 31).
3. **Ezekiel:** Prophesied to the exiles in Babylon, employing vivid symbolic actions to illustrate divine judgments and eventual restoration. His visions of God's glory departing from the temple and returning again highlight spiritual truths about God's presence (Ezekiel 1, 8–10, 37).

4. **Minor Prophets:** This collection includes a range of voices—from Hosea's portrayal of Israel's unfaithfulness and God's steadfast love (Hosea 1–3) to Malachi's call for renewed faithfulness after the return from exile (Malachi 1–4). Their themes vary, yet all emphasize the demands of covenant fidelity and divine justice.

Collectively, these prophetic writings paint a picture of a God who is deeply invested in the ethical and spiritual well-being of His people. The prophets did not merely provide moral guidelines; they stood as a conscience for the nation, urging repentance and underscoring both the consequences of disobedience and the blessings of returning to God.

2.1.4 Divine Calling and Commissioning

Almost every prophetic figure in the Old Testament recounts a defining moment of divine calling. This often included a revelation of God's holiness and a humbling sense of one's own inadequacy. For example, Isaiah's calling involved a dramatic vision of the Lord seated on a throne, attended by seraphim crying out, "Holy, holy, holy" (Isaiah 6:1–5). Overwhelmed by his own "unclean lips," Isaiah only found readiness to speak for the Lord after receiving purification with coal from the altar.

Jeremiah's call narrative (Jeremiah 1:4–10) likewise portrays a reluctance rooted in his youth and feelings of unworthiness. God reassured him with the words, "Do not say, 'I am only a youth,' for to all to whom I send you, you shall go... Do not be afraid... for I am with you." Such commissioning accounts highlight that prophets did not volunteer for their office based on natural inclination or ambition; rather, they were chosen and empowered by God, often to their own surprise or dismay.

2.1.5 Responsibilities within the Covenant Community

The overarching mission of prophets was to restore and maintain the right relationship between God and His people.

While priests facilitated worship through sacrifices, the prophet's role involved the following responsibilities:

1. **Proclaiming God's Will:** This included revealing divine directives, admonitions, or judgments to individuals or communities. Sometimes, these proclamations were warnings—e.g., Jonah's terse message to Nineveh (Jonah 3:4)—while others were consolations, such as the prophecies of comfort in Isaiah 40–41.

2. **Calling for Repentance:** Idolatry was a recurring issue in ancient Israel, and prophets addressed it consistently. Elijah's dramatic confrontation with the prophets of Baal on Mount Carmel (1 Kings 18) stands as a quintessential example of a prophet calling the people to abandon false gods and return to Yahweh.

3. **Interceding on Behalf of the People:** Prophets like Moses and Samuel interceded earnestly for Israel, pleading that God's wrath might be turned away when the nation sinned. Their intercessory prayers reveal the compassionate side of prophetic ministry as they stood in the gap between divine holiness and human fallibility.

4. **Confronting Kings and Leaders:** In societies where monarchs wielded immense power, prophets functioned as a check and balance. Nathan's bold rebuke of King David after the Bathsheba incident (2 Samuel 12) and Elijah's confrontation of King Ahab (1 Kings 21) both illustrate how prophets were compelled to speak truth to power, regardless of personal risk.

5. **Teaching and Guidance:** While not always the main focus, many prophets also offered instruction about living in righteousness, upholding justice, and caring for society's vulnerable members. Passages like Isaiah 58:6–7, which emphasize genuine acts of compassion over mere ritual fasting, show the prophetic concern for ethical living.

2.1.6 The Unique Relationship with the Holy Spirit

Although the Old Testament does not describe the indwelling of the Holy Spirit in believers the same way the New Testament does, it emphasizes that the Spirit of the Lord rested upon or filled prophets to enable their ministry. Ezekiel frequently mentions being lifted or carried by the Spirit (Ezekiel 2:2; 3:12–14), while Micah asserts, "But as for me, I am filled with power, with the Spirit of the Lord, and with justice and might, to declare to Jacob his transgression" (Micah 3:8).

This endowment of the Spirit served to authenticate the prophet's message, ensuring that it came from God rather than from human reasoning. It also undergirded the prophetic calling with supernatural boldness. The capacity to speak oracles that cut through cultural norms and challenge the status quo could only be sustained by divine empowerment. The prophet's dependence on the Holy Spirit was integral to delivering accurate messages, bearing emotional burdens, and standing firm in the face of opposition.

2.2 The Burden of the Oracle

2.2.1 Understanding "Burden" in the Prophetic Context

The Old Testament often employs the Hebrew word *massa'* (מַשָּׂא) to refer to an oracle of judgment or a prophetic pronouncement, sometimes translated as "burden." This choice of terminology conveys the weight of responsibility borne by the prophet. Carrying the "burden of the Lord" meant delivering messages that were not always welcomed and could elicit strong reactions—anger, rejection, persecution, or even threats of death. Unlike modern notions of "burden" as a mere inconvenience, this biblical sense underscores something that cannot be lightly cast aside; it is a divine mandate requiring faithfulness regardless of personal cost.

2.2.2 Emotional and Spiritual Weight

Many biblical narratives portray prophets wrestling with deep anguish over the messages they must deliver. Jeremiah is a prime example. Dubbed the "weeping prophet," he poured out his sorrow in laments because he felt compelled to announce the destruction of Jerusalem and the exile of its people. In Jeremiah 20:9, he describes God's word as a "fire shut up in [his] bones," illustrating the inescapable inner compulsion to speak despite the pain and persecution it brought him.

This emotional turmoil is not confined to Jeremiah. In 1 Kings 19, Elijah flees into the wilderness, overwhelmed by despair and fear after his dramatic victory on Mount Carmel. Even though he had witnessed God's power, the relentless opposition from Jezebel and the broader culture weighed heavily upon him. This account reveals the profound isolation and vulnerability prophets often faced. Their calling set them apart, sometimes leaving them with few allies among the very people they sought to help.

2.2.3 Prophetic Actions and Symbolic Gestures

One noteworthy way prophets expressed the burden they carried was through symbolic actions or "sign-acts." These dramatic enactments were intended to communicate God's messages in a visceral manner, leaving a memorable impression on the observers. For example:

- **Isaiah** walked barefoot and naked for three years as a sign against Egypt and Cush (Isaiah 20:2–4). This shocking action illustrated the shame and humiliation that would come upon those nations.
- **Ezekiel** constructed a model of Jerusalem under siege and lay on his side for prolonged periods to symbolize the years of judgment upon Israel and Judah (Ezekiel 4).
- **Jeremiah** wore a yoke on his neck to demonstrate the coming Babylonian captivity (Jeremiah 27–28).

These prophetic gestures served as physical embodiments of the oracle, reinforcing the message's seriousness and inevitability. However, performing such acts could also invite ridicule and further alienation, compounding the prophet's burden.

2.2.4 The Loneliness of the Prophetic Call

Another dimension of the prophet's burden is relational estrangement. Because prophets often delivered messages of rebuke or dire warning, they were seldom popular. When confronting national sins—such as injustice toward the poor, corrupt leadership, or rampant idolatry—prophets placed themselves in direct opposition to societal norms. As a result, many prophets experienced isolation from their communities.

Jeremiah's complaints in Jeremiah 15:17–18 depict how he felt ostracized: "I did not sit in the company of revelers... Your hand was upon me in wrath... Why is my pain unceasing?" This sense of separation was not merely a social byproduct; it also stemmed from the deep spiritual calling that set the prophet apart for God's purposes. The vow of dedication or the intensity of the divine commission often meant that normal familial or social bonds were overshadowed by the urgency of proclaiming God's message.

2.2.5 The Cost of Faithful Delivery

The cost of carrying and delivering the oracle could be extremely high, sometimes endangering the prophet's very life. While some, like Nathan or Gad, seemed to move relatively freely in royal courts, others faced threats and persecution. Tradition holds that Isaiah was martyred under King Manasseh. Jeremiah was repeatedly imprisoned and narrowly escaped execution (Jeremiah 38). Zechariah, son of Jehoiada, was stoned for rebuking the people's transgressions (2 Chronicles 24:20–21). Over and over, prophets discovered that speaking truth to power and exposing widespread corruption incurred severe consequences.

Despite these hardships, the faithful prophets remained resolute, driven by a conviction that God's word must be spoken regardless of personal repercussions. The willingness to pay such a price underlines the authenticity of their calling. It also illustrates why the office of prophet was uniquely challenging: genuine prophets could not simply choose to be silent when the message of the Lord burned within them like fire.

2.3 False Oracles and Deception

2.3.1 Prevalence of False Prophets in Israel's History

One might imagine that a community so thoroughly grounded in the covenant worship of Yahweh would naturally reject any voice that did not align with the divine will. However, the Old Testament reveals that false prophets often outnumbered the true ones and were sometimes more influential, at least temporarily. This dynamic is evident in the confrontation between Elijah and the prophets of Baal on Mount Carmel (1 Kings 18). While Elijah stood alone, King Ahab and Queen Jezebel had fostered an environment where hundreds of false prophets flourished. These "prophets" presumably told the king whatever he wanted to hear, reinforcing political agendas rather than conveying the genuine word of the Lord.

Similarly, the prophet Micaiah stands out in 1 Kings 22. King Ahab's official prophets unanimously declared victory in battle, but Micaiah, a lone voice of genuine prophecy, contradicted them, foretelling defeat. Furious, Ahab had Micaiah imprisoned. This incident illustrates how leaders often surrounded themselves with "yes-men" prophets who offered comforting but deceptive oracles. It also underscores how the popularity of a prophecy does not guarantee its authenticity.

2.3.2 The Danger of Divination and Syncretism

False prophecy in ancient Israel was frequently linked with the practices of surrounding nations. The Lord repeatedly warned Israel not to consult mediums, necromancers, or pagan diviners (Deuteronomy 18:9–14). Such practices not only demonstrated distrust in the Lord's guidance but also opened the door to spiritual deception. Some false prophets engaged in methods similar to pagan soothsaying, claiming to speak for Yahweh while actually drawing from occult traditions or personal agendas.

Syncretism—the blending of worship of Yahweh with other gods—fueled this problem. Instead of remaining faithful to the covenant, many Israelites erected high places and Asherah poles, integrating pagan elements into their worship. False prophets capitalized on this syncretic environment, justifying idolatrous practices and refusing to challenge the moral compromises that came with them. As a result, their oracles led people away from true worship rather than toward repentance and renewal.

2.3.3 Criteria for Distinguishing True and False Prophecy

The Old Testament sets forth explicit guidelines to help the covenant community discern a genuine prophet from a counterfeit. Two key passages stand out: Deuteronomy 13:1–5 and Deuteronomy 18:20–22. These passages highlight that even if a prophet's sign or wonder appears to come true, the real litmus test is whether the message aligns with the worship of Yahweh and the covenant law.

1. **Fidelity to God's Character and Commandments:** A true prophet always upholds the exclusive worship of the Lord. If someone performs a miraculous sign but then urges the people to follow other gods, that individual is labeled false, regardless of the sign's apparent authenticity (Deuteronomy 13:2–4).
2. **Accuracy of Fulfilled Predictions:** Deuteronomy 18:21–22 indicates that if a prophet speaks in the name of the Lord and the word does not come to pass, "that is a word that the Lord has not spoken." This straightforward criterion underscores that God does not err; if a message truly comes from Him, it will be fulfilled in its proper time and context. That said, some prophecies are long-range, so discernment requires patience and humility.

3. **Moral and Ethical Fruit:** While not explicitly stated in the aforementioned passages, the overarching biblical narrative suggests that true prophets also embody moral integrity. Their lifestyle, though not perfect, generally reflects submission to God. By contrast, false prophets often pursue personal gain or align themselves too closely with corrupt rulers to maintain favor and power (Micah 3:5–11).

2.3.4 The Role of the Community and Leadership

In theory, the covenant community was supposed to heed these guidelines, rooting out false prophets to protect the integrity of worship. However, biblical history reveals that the reality was far more complex. Kings sometimes used false prophets to legitimize unjust policies. The common people might prefer reassuring falsehoods over the hard truths delivered by genuine prophets. Indeed, Jeremiah 5:31 famously critiques a populace that loves to hear deceptions: "The prophets prophesy falsely, and the priests rule at their direction; my people love to have it so."

Nonetheless, a faithful remnant often emerged to challenge this status quo. Figures like Elijah, Elisha, Hosea, and Amos stood firm, proclaiming messages of judgment, repentance, and hope. These prophets sometimes found support among a minority of believers who recognized the voice of God in their utterances. In this sense, the responsibility for discerning oracles lay with both religious and lay communities. Discerning hearts were capable of testing the spirits and messages, ensuring that what was spoken truly aligned with God's covenant standards (cf. 1 John 4:1, although that reference belongs to the New Testament era, the principle of testing prophecy is broadly echoed throughout Scripture).

2.3.5 Consequences of Following False Oracles

Succumbing to deceptive messages did not merely result in theological confusion; it carried profound social and political ramifications. Time and again, Israel's spiritual infidelity, fueled by the words of false prophets, led to national decline, foreign oppression, or even exile. For instance, Jeremiah warned of Babylon's imminent conquest, but false prophets insisted on assurances of peace and security (Jeremiah 6:14; 14:13–16). Clinging to these comforting illusions, the leaders refused to repent or prepare. As a result, Jerusalem fell to Babylon, and countless lives were devastated.

In the Old Testament perspective, turning to false prophets amounted to rejecting God's rightful place as the sovereign Lord. Consequently, the blessings promised in the covenant were forfeited, replaced by curses that were themselves clearly spelled out in the Torah (Leviticus 26; Deuteronomy 28). Although the historical circumstances differ in modern times, the underlying principle remains pertinent: heeding voices that promise easy prosperity or success without requiring genuine repentance and obedience to God often leads to spiritual disillusionment and moral decay.

In conclusion, prophets were the vessels through which God's oracles reached His people, whether those messages called for repentance, offered comfort, or foretold events on the horizon. Far from being passive mediums, these men and women actively participated in God's redemptive narrative— challenging kings, guiding national decisions, and frequently paying a severe personal price for their faithfulness.

Understanding the prophetic role entails appreciating both the high calling and the deep burdens that came with it. The biblical writers do not romanticize the life of the prophet; instead, they depict it as one of struggle, isolation, and often suffering. Yet this suffering had purpose: through the prophets, God relentlessly pursued His people, urging them to return to covenant obedience. From Moses to Malachi, and from Deborah to Jeremiah, each prophet added fresh layers to the tapestry of Israel's spiritual heritage, providing a moral and theological compass that pointed to the righteousness and mercy of Yahweh.

The tendency for false oracles—whether emerging from self-serving motives, political manipulations, or outright idolatrous practices—emphasized the necessity of discernment within the community. Properly discerning God's true messages required adherence to divine standards: alignment with God's revealed character, fulfillment of predictions, and moral credibility. When these criteria were ignored, the resulting deception triggered dire consequences for individuals and nations alike.

Ultimately, the legacy of these Old Testament prophets extends far beyond their historical context, reminding readers today that divine communication is both a sacred gift and a serious responsibility. When God speaks—whether through Scripture, the conviction of the Holy Spirit, or other means—it is incumbent upon His people to listen with reverence, test what they hear with faithfulness to His revealed will, and respond with obedience that honors the One who continues to guide and correct His children.

Chapter 3: Jesus – The Living Oracle

For centuries, the people of God waited in hope for the ultimate revelation of the divine Word. Prophets had come and gone, carrying messages that simultaneously warned, directed, and comforted the covenant community. Yet even the greatest of these prophets spoke of a future time when God would make Himself known in an unprecedented way— when the "Word" would take on a form more accessible, tangible, and immediate than ever before.

The Gospels declare that this longing was fulfilled in Jesus Christ, the Son of God, who entered human history as both fully divine and fully human. In Him, the voice of heaven was not just heard; it was seen, touched, and intimately experienced. Jesus did not merely speak the Word; He *is* the Word—God's ultimate communication of grace, truth, and redemptive power. This chapter explores how Jesus' identity as the incarnate Word transforms the nature of divine revelation, underscores the authority of His teaching, and fulfills prophetic anticipations that stretch back to the earliest promises in Scripture.

3.1 Christ as the Word Made Flesh

3.1.1 The Eternal Word Enters Time

The Gospel of John opens with a staggering declaration: "In the beginning was the Word, and the Word was with God, and the Word was God" (John 1:1). The Greek term translated as "Word" is *logos*, which carries a rich cluster of meanings in both Hellenistic and Jewish thought. In philosophical contexts, *logos* could imply the rational principle that orders the cosmos, while in biblical contexts, it resonates with the concept of God's spoken and creative Word as seen in Genesis 1, where God speaks the universe into existence.

By identifying Jesus as this *logos*, John makes a bold assertion: Jesus does not merely come to deliver a divine message; He Himself is the message. Before creation, before any prophets arose, the Word existed in eternal fellowship with the Father. Thus, Jesus' origin is not bound to human genealogy or historical circumstance; He is pre-existent and co-eternal with God. This truth lays the foundation for His unparalleled authority as the supreme "oracle," the One who embodies God's communication in His very being.

3.1.2 The Miracle of the Incarnation

John 1:14 adds another dimension, stating, "And the Word became flesh and dwelt among us." This single verse encapsulates the heart of the Christian faith: The transcendent God entered the sphere of human experience by taking on human nature. In doing so, God's communication to humanity became more than words inscribed on tablets of stone or scrolls of parchment. Instead, it was personally demonstrated in the life, teaching, death, and resurrection of Jesus.

The Greek term behind "dwelt" (*eskēnōsen*) literally means "tabernacled" or "pitched a tent." This alludes to the Old Testament Tabernacle, where God's presence resided among the Israelites (Exodus 25:8–9). Now, rather than dwelling behind a veil or manifesting in a tent, God chose to make His dwelling in human flesh. This radical condescension signifies divine intimacy and accessibility. No longer is divine revelation restricted to particular holy sites or religious rituals. In Jesus, people encountered the fullness of God's truth and compassion in a living, breathing person.

3.1.3 The Glory of God Revealed

John completes his statement in 1:14 by affirming that those who beheld Jesus "have seen his glory, glory as of the only Son from the Father, full of grace and truth." Glory (Greek: *doxa*) in Scripture frequently refers to the manifestation of God's splendor and holiness. In the Old Testament, this glory appeared in a cloud on Mount Sinai (Exodus 24:16) and in the Most Holy Place of the tabernacle (Exodus 40:34–35). With the coming of Christ, the glory that once made Moses hide his face (Exodus 34:33) becomes visible in a form that draws, rather than repels, mankind.

Yet this glory is not merely an external radiance. The "grace and truth" Jesus embodies indicate the depth of God's character. Grace represents God's unmerited favor, the free gift of salvation, while truth speaks to the reliability and faithfulness of His promises. Through Jesus, believers witness how these attributes converge, forming a perfect reflection of the Father's heart.

3.1.4 The Bridge Between Heaven and Earth

Because Jesus is fully God and fully man, He uniquely bridges the gap between the divine and the human. The Scriptures identify Him as the only mediator who can reconcile humanity to God (1 Timothy 2:5). His dual nature means He can authentically speak on God's behalf (since He is God) and fully empathize with human frailty (since He is man).

This mediatorial role is central to understanding Jesus as the "Living Oracle." In the Hebrew tradition, prophets like Moses or Isaiah served as intermediaries, conveying divine messages. Yet, each prophet remained merely human, bound by their own limitations and prone to personal sin or misunderstanding. In Jesus, the Word is perfectly communicated without distortion, as there is no moral or existential distance between the message and its source. Christ's every word and deed reveals the Father's will.

3 1.5 Fulfilling and Surpassing Previous Revelations

Hebrews 1:1–2 famously declares, "Long ago, at many times and in many ways, God spoke to our fathers by the prophets, but in these last days he has spoken to us by his Son." The author of Hebrews underscores that while God certainly communicated through Old Testament prophets, Jesus represents the culmination and climax of all previous revelation. What God had expressed in fragments and shadows throughout history is fully manifested in Christ.

This does not invalidate prior revelations; rather, it confirms and completes them. In Jesus, the covenant promises, the sacrificial system, and the prophetic messages pointing to salvation find their ultimate realization. His teachings, character, and work interpret the Scriptures in their true light— demonstrating that the entire biblical narrative anticipates and converges upon Him.

3.2 The Teachings and Declarations of Jesus

Even a cursory reading of the Gospels reveals that Jesus taught with an authority distinct from that of any other figure in Scripture. Crowds were stunned by His words, remarking that He spoke not like the scribes but "as one who had authority" (Matthew 7:29). While Old Testament prophets typically prefaced their statements with "Thus says the LORD," Jesus often began with "Truly, truly, I say to you" (e.g., John 6:47). This shift indicates that He is speaking directly from His own divine prerogative, underscoring His identity as the Living Oracle.

3.2.1 The Authority of His Words

Throughout the Gospels, people marvel at Jesus' teachings because they do not rely on external sources for validation.

Unlike the rabbis of His day, who frequently cited earlier teachers to establish credibility, Jesus' words stand on their own. Passages like John 7:14–18 illustrate that Jesus's authority comes "from the one who sent [Him]," aligning His message perfectly with the Father's will.

This intrinsic authority pervades every dimension of His teaching. When confronted by religious leaders, Jesus does not back down or present His statements as mere interpretations; rather, He frames them as definitive truth that demands a response. For example, in John 8:58, He declares, "Before Abraham was, I am." By appropriating the divine name "I AM" (Exodus 3:14), Jesus claims an eternal existence and equality with God, prompting shock and even attempts on His life by those who consider this blasphemous (John 8:59).

3.2.2 The Sermon on the Mount

Among the most famous expositions of Jesus' teaching is the Sermon on the Mount (Matthew 5–7). Often regarded as the ethical heart of the Gospel, this sermon outlines values and principles that invert conventional human wisdom. Rather than celebrating power, wealth, or external religiosity, Jesus blesses the poor in spirit, those who mourn, and the meek (Matthew 5:3–5). His radical instructions include loving one's enemies, turning the other cheek, and storing treasures in heaven rather than on earth (Matthew 5:44, 5:39, 6:19–20).

3.2.2.1 Fulfilling the Law, Not Abolishing It

A pivotal statement in the sermon appears in Matthew 5:17, where Jesus insists He has not come to abolish the Law or the Prophets but to fulfill them. This claim further underscores His identity as the One who brings completion to earlier covenantal teachings. By emphasizing internal righteousness over mere external adherence (Matthew 5:21–48), Jesus reorients the Mosaic regulations around the spirit behind them.

3.2.2.2 A Higher Righteousness

Another hallmark of the Sermon on the Mount is Jesus' call for a "righteousness [that] exceeds that of the scribes and Pharisees" (Matthew 5:20). This elevated moral vision is not meant to promote self-righteousness but to push believers toward genuine transformation of the heart. As the Living Oracle, Jesus ties every aspect of ethical living to the nature of God, urging His followers to "be perfect, as your heavenly Father is perfect" (Matthew 5:48).

3.2.3 The Kingdom Parables

Jesus frequently used parables—short, illustrative stories—to convey the nature of God's kingdom. Each parable acts as a self-contained "oracle," challenging listeners to see the world from a divine perspective. These stories often subvert common assumptions, highlighting how God's values differ radically from human conventions.

3.2.3.1 The Purpose of Parables

Matthew 13:10–17 clarifies that Jesus taught in parables both to reveal and to conceal truth. To those spiritually receptive, the stories illuminate profound mysteries about God's reign. However, to those unwilling to humble themselves, the same parables remain obscure. This dynamic underscores that responding to Jesus' teaching requires not merely intellectual assent but a posture of faith and repentance.

3.2.3.2 Samples of Kingdom Realities

- **The Parable of the Sower (Mark 4:1–20; Matthew 13:3–23):** Depicts different types of hearts that receive or reject the Word. Some are shallow or distracted, while others are fertile ground for spiritual growth.
- **The Parable of the Prodigal Son (Luke 15:11–32):** Illustrates God's grace and willingness to restore repentant sinners, reversing cultural expectations about forgiveness and family honor.

- **The Parable of the Mustard Seed (Matthew 13:31–32):** Shows how the kingdom of heaven starts small yet grows exponentially, emphasizing God's surprising ways of establishing His reign.

Through these parables, Jesus conveys that the kingdom of God is both "already" and "not yet." It is breaking into history through His presence and works, yet it will only be fully consummated in the future. Thus, the parables invite hearers to participate in the kingdom's unfolding reality by aligning their lives with God's will.

3.2.4 The "I AM" Statements

One of the most striking aspects of Jesus' teaching is His use of the "I AM" formula, particularly recorded in the Gospel of John. These statements do more than identify Jesus with certain metaphors; they link Him directly to Yahweh, the self-revealing God of the Old Testament (Exodus 3:14). Each "I AM" statement reveals an aspect of His mission and character:

- **I am the Bread of Life (John 6:35):** Jesus presents Himself as the ultimate sustenance, capable of satisfying humanity's spiritual hunger.
- **I am the Light of the World (John 8:12):** He dispels darkness, guiding those who follow Him into truth.
- **I am the Door (John 10:7–9):** He is the only legitimate entry point to salvation and security.
- **I am the Good Shepherd (John 10:11–14):** Jesus cares for His flock, even laying down His life for them.
- **I am the Resurrection and the Life (John 11:25):** He holds power over death, guaranteeing eternal life to believers.
- **I am the Way, the Truth, and the Life (John 14:6):** Jesus is the exclusive path to the Father, the very embodiment of truth, and the source of true life.
- **I am the True Vine (John 15:1):** Union with Him is vital for spiritual fruitfulness.

These declarations emphasize Jesus' divine identity and His sufficiency to meet all human needs. They also challenge any notion of Jesus as merely a moral teacher or prophet, He presents Himself as God-in the-flesh, upon whom eternal destinies hinge.

3.3 Jesus' Prophecies and Fulfillments

Jesus' identity as the Living Oracle is further confirmed by His prophetic role. Though He is far more than a prophet—being the very source of the prophetic Word—He nevertheless delivered specific predictions that were fulfilled in remarkable ways. These prophecies ranged from short-term forecasts to long-term eschatological revelations, all of which highlight His omniscience and sovereign authority.

3.3.1 Prophecies about His Death and Resurrection

Repeatedly throughout the Gospels, Jesus foretells His own arrest, suffering, death, and resurrection. He does so with increasing clarity, preparing His disciples for what lies ahead even though they struggle to comprehend it.

- **Mark 8:31**: Jesus begins teaching that "the Son of Man must suffer many things and be rejected… and after three days rise again."
- **Matthew 16:21–23**: Peter resists the notion of a suffering Messiah, prompting Jesus to rebuke him for setting his mind on human rather than divine concerns.
- **Luke 18:31–33**: Jesus predicts specific details of His passion, including mockery, shame, and His eventual triumph over death.

3.3.1.1 The Sign of Jonah

In Matthew 12:39–40, Jesus references the prophet Jonah's three days in the belly of the fish as a foreshadowing of His own burial and resurrection. This "sign of Jonah" underscores the divine plan that was woven into the Old Testament narrative. Jesus's ability to correlate Jonah's experience with

His impending sacrifice and resurrection further demonstrates His comprehensive understanding of Scripture as it points to His redemptive work.

3.3.1.2 Fulfillment in the Resurrection

The climax of Jesus' prophetic utterances about His death is, of course, the empty tomb. All four Gospels affirm that Jesus physically rose from the dead on the third day, a reality that changed the course of history. The resurrection vindicated His claim to divine sonship (Romans 1:4) and validated every word He had spoken. If Jesus had not risen, His teachings would be relegated to a collection of ethical instructions from a charismatic leader. Instead, the resurrection confirms that He is the Living Lord, whose prophetic words stand forever.

3.3.2 The Destruction of the Temple

One of the most notable prophecies Jesus made during His earthly ministry concerned the fate of the Jerusalem temple. Recorded in passages such as Matthew 24:1–2, Mark 13:1–2, and Luke 21:5–6, Jesus foretold that not one stone of the magnificent temple complex would be left upon another.

At the time, the temple stood as the cultural and religious centerpiece of Jewish worship, originally constructed under Solomon, reconstructed during the post-exilic period, and massively expanded by King Herod. The notion that this grand structure could be obliterated seemed almost unimaginable. Yet in AD 70—less than four decades after Jesus uttered these words—the Roman armies besieged Jerusalem and destroyed the temple, fulfilling Jesus' prophecy with chilling precision.

3.3.2.1 Significance of the Temple's Destruction

From a theological standpoint, the temple's destruction signified a monumental shift. No longer would worship be confined to a specific geographic location or ritual system (cf. John 4:21–24). Through His death and resurrection, Jesus inaugurated a new covenant in which worshipers approach

God through faith in Him, the true and living sanctuary (Hebrews 9:11–14). The demise of the earthly temple underscored Christ's role as the ultimate high priest who mediates between God and humanity.

3.3.2.2 Validation of Christ's Prophetic Authority

Jesus' accurate prediction of such a massive historical event underscores His standing as the Living Oracle. This prophecy was not a vague statement but a concrete description of what would happen to a major religious institution. The temple's downfall confirmed the authority of His pronouncements and validated His larger teachings about the nature of the kingdom of God—a kingdom not rooted in the external trappings of religion but in the transformative work of the Holy Spirit.

3.3.3 The Promise of His Return

Another sphere of Jesus' prophetic declarations concerns His second coming and the consummation of history. In passages such as Matthew 24, Mark 13, and Luke 21, often referred to collectively as the "Olivet Discourse," Jesus outlines signs that will precede His return, including wars, natural disasters, and widespread spiritual deception.

3.3.3.1 A Future-Oriented Oracle

Whereas many of the Old Testament prophets pointed forward to a messianic age, Jesus points beyond His earthly ministry to a future event when He will return in power and glory. This return is not described as a symbolic or purely spiritual phenomenon but as a literal, visible occurrence (Matthew 24:30; Acts 1:11). He instructs His followers to remain vigilant, emphasizing that the exact day or hour is unknown, and encouraging a life of readiness and faithfulness (Matthew 24:42–44).

3.3.3.2 The Continuation of His Mission

The promise of Jesus's return has profound implications for believers. It assures them that history has a purposeful trajectory, moving toward the full realization of God's kingdom. Christians throughout the centuries have found hope and motivation in this oracle, enduring persecution, suffering, and the trials of life with the expectation that Christ will set all things right. Moreover, the knowledge that Jesus will come again encourages moral and spiritual vigilance, calling believers to live in a manner worthy of His name.

In Jesus Christ, the Word of God is no longer an abstract concept or a distant pronouncement delivered through human intermediaries. He is *Emmanuel*, God with us—God speaking to us, walking among us, suffering for us, and ultimately triumphing over sin and death on our behalf. As the "Living Oracle," Jesus perfectly discloses the Father's character, will, and eternal purposes.

1. **He Is the Word Made Flesh**: The incarnation of the eternal *logos* in human form signifies the pinnacle of divine self-revelation. No longer limited to written texts or distant voices, God now communicates through a Person who embodies the fullness of grace and truth.
2. **His Teachings Carry Absolute Authority**: Whether through the Sermon on the Mount, parables, or the "I AM" statements, Jesus imparts divine truth with a directness and finality that surpasses all earlier prophetic voices. His call to a higher righteousness and genuine heart transformation resonates throughout the ages, drawing people out of religious formalism into a living relationship with God.
3. **His Prophecies Validate His Identity**: The predictions Jesus made—about His own death and resurrection, the destruction of the temple, and His eventual return—demonstrate His prophetic role. Their fulfillment in history (and their expected future fulfillment) confirm Him as the reliable, sovereign Oracle whose words cannot fail.
4. **He Fulfills and Surpasses All Previous Revelations**: Building upon the foundation of the Law and the Prophets, Jesus completes the scriptural narrative and inaugurates a new covenant. Every

promise in Scripture finds its "yes" and "amen" in Him (2 Corinthians 1:20).

In conclusion, as the Living Oracle, He does more than point to God's Word; He *is* God's Word—embodied, active, and powerful to save.

The implications of recognizing Jesus in this way are manifold. It means that to know God, one must know Christ; to hear from God, one must heed Christ's teachings; and to live in communion with God, one must embrace the transforming presence of Christ. Far from being relegated to an ancient text, Jesus' voice continues to speak across centuries, calling every generation to repentance, faith, and a life shaped by divine love.

For believers, cherishing Jesus as the Living Oracle cultivates a faith rooted in wonder, humility, and boldness: wonder at the mystery of the incarnation, humility at the depth of God's condescension, and boldness because His resurrection power is available to all who trust in Him. Thus, while earlier prophets faithfully transmitted God's words, and while Scripture remains the inspired record of divine revelation, it is in Jesus that the written Word becomes flesh, rendering God's message not just heard but personally encountered.

Even today, millions testify that the teachings of Jesus still resonate with uncanny relevance, addressing deep questions about purpose, morality, identity, and destiny. Whether it is His invitation to experience rest for weary souls (Matthew 11:28–30) or His promise of eternal life (John 3:16), Jesus' words act as a divine summons, confronting every person with a decision: will we receive the Word and be transformed, or will we dismiss it and continue in spiritual darkness?

Chapter 4: The Apostolic Oracle – Speaking the Mysteries

From the very outset of Christianity, the apostles held a unique and authoritative position. As direct witnesses to Christ's resurrection—and, in the case of Paul, one who encountered the risen Jesus in a dramatic conversion experience (Acts 9:1–19)—these men were commissioned to make disciples of all nations (Matthew 28:19–20) and to build up the body of believers through teaching, leadership, and the discernment of truth. In a real sense, they became the "oracles" of the New Testament era, speaking forth under divine inspiration to unveil God's redemptive plan in Christ.

The apostolic voice echoes throughout the Book of Acts and resonates in the epistolary writings that form a substantial portion of the New Testament. These texts do more than recount historical events or outline theological propositions; they bear the weight of divine authority, illuminating the spiritual realities hidden for ages but now revealed in Christ (Colossians 1:26). Through the apostles, the Holy Spirit offered directives that shaped Christian doctrine, worship, and communal life—a pattern that continues to guide believers nearly two millennia later.

An especially rich dimension of this apostolic ministry involves the concept of "mysteries." In the New Testament, the word "mystery" (Greek: *mystērion*) does not imply an unsolvable riddle but rather a sacred secret that God has chosen to disclose in His perfect time. While Old Testament figures saw only shadows of the Messianic age, the apostles now proclaimed the fullness of that hidden plan, centering on the person and work of Jesus Christ. Their inspired writings, teachings, and testimonies thus serve as the final scaffolding upon which the Church stands—a continuation of the divine oracle that began in creation, ran through the Old Testament prophetic tradition, climaxed in Jesus, and was further expounded by His closest emissaries.

4.1 The Apostles and the Early Church

4.1.1 Birth of the Apostolic Age

The apostolic era began in earnest with the outpouring of the Holy Spirit at Pentecost (Acts 2). Following Jesus' ascension, about 120 believers (Acts 1:15) gathered in prayer until the Spirit descended upon them in "tongues of fire" (Acts 2:3). This dramatic event empowered them to speak in other languages, symbolizing the Gospel's reach to every nation. It also signaled the inauguration of a new phase in God's redemptive history, where the apostolic community would serve as the vital channel of divine revelation.

Peter's sermon on that day (Acts 2:14–36) can be viewed as the inaugural apostolic oracle. Drawing on Old Testament passages—most notably from the prophet Joel—Peter explained that the long-awaited outpouring of the Spirit had come, fulfilling God's promise for the last days (Joel 2:28–32). He also declared Jesus as both "Lord and Christ," proclaiming His death and resurrection as the pivotal acts for humanity's salvation. In response to this Spirit-empowered message, about three thousand people were converted (Acts 2:41). The apostolic Church—founded on preaching, fellowship, breaking of bread, and prayer (Acts 2:42)—rose as a living testament to the ongoing work of the Holy Spirit and the veracity of the Gospel.

This early growth and communal life display a powerful pattern: God moves mightily when His Word is faithfully proclaimed by His chosen vessels. The apostles, once ordinary fishermen, tax collectors, and political zealots, were now entrusted with an oracle of unprecedented magnitude: the revelation of Jesus as the crucified and risen Messiah, and the invitation for all humanity to participate in the grace of His new covenant.

4.1.2 Apostolic Authority and Its Confirmation

An essential characteristic of the apostles was their divine commissioning by Jesus. Luke 6:13 notes that Jesus personally selected the Twelve, calling them "apostles," which in Greek literally means "sent ones." Later, after Judas' betrayal and death, Matthias was chosen through prayerful discernment to maintain the number of the Twelve (Acts 1:23–26). Paul would later join their ranks through a unique encounter with the risen Christ.

Throughout the Book of Acts, apostolic authority is evidenced by signs and wonders. In Acts 3:1–10, Peter and John heal a man lame from birth, a miraculous sign that sparks curiosity and invites Peter to deliver another powerful sermon (Acts 3:11–26). Similarly, Acts 5:12–16 recounts how the sick were healed when Peter's shadow fell upon them. Such miracles functioned not as ends in themselves but as confirmations of the divine truth the apostles proclaimed. By displaying supernatural power, God effectively authenticated the apostolic message, underscoring that their words were not mere human opinions but the oracles of God (Hebrews 2:3–4).

Apostolic authority also extended to ecclesial matters. Acts 6:1–7 depicts how the apostles guided administrative decisions, such as the distribution of food to widows, ensuring that no group was neglected. In Acts 8:14–17, Peter and John traveled to Samaria to validate the Samaritan believers' faith, praying for them to receive the Holy Spirit. Perhaps most notably, Acts 15 describes the Jerusalem Council—a pivotal moment where apostolic leaders, together with elders, deliberated whether Gentile converts should be circumcised and adhere to Mosaic customs. The council's final letter, drafted and dispatched to the Gentile believers, carried weight as an authoritative pronouncement shaped by the Holy Spirit's guidance (Acts 15:28–29). This event highlights the apostles' function as living conduits of divine guidance, clarifying doctrinal issues in ways that would continue to shape Christian faith and practice.

4.1.3 Apostolic Preaching in the Book of Acts

The Book of Acts, sometimes called "The Acts of the Apostles," can be read as a collection of apostolic oracles in action. From Peter's early sermons to Paul's speeches before Gentile audiences, each proclamation further reveals how the good news transcended ethnic, cultural, and geographical boundaries. While each apostle brought a distinct personality, background, and methodology, a few common threads recur in their messages:

1. **Christ-Centered Focus**: Whether addressing Jews in Jerusalem or Gentiles in Athens, the apostles consistently foregrounded Jesus' identity as the crucified and risen Savior. Sermons typically underscored Christ's fulfillment of Old Testament prophecies, His atoning death, and the promise of eternal life through faith in Him (Acts 2:22–24; 13:26–39).
2. **Call to Repentance and Baptism**: Apostolic preaching universally exhorted listeners to repent of sin, turn to God, and publicly attest their faith through baptism (Acts 2:38; 8:12). This transformation signaled entrance into the covenant community of believers and acceptance of the Spirit's regenerative work.
3. **Verification through Scripture**: Particularly when addressing Jewish audiences, apostles appealed to the Law, the Prophets, and the Psalms as testimonies

to Jesus' messiahship (Acts 2:25–28; 13:27–41). Their arguments exemplify how the Old Testament revelations anticipate and confirm the new covenant reality manifested in Christ.

4. **Universality of the Gospel**: Through divine visions (Acts 10:9–16) and providential encounters (Acts 8:26–40), the apostles realized the Gospel's universal scope. No person, whether Jewish, Samaritan, or Gentile, was excluded from God's redemptive plan, as long as they responded to the apostolic message with faith.

This preaching pattern reveals the theological core of the early Church and illustrates how the apostles, inspired by the Spirit, became "living oracles" of the new era. Their verbal witness, coupled with their exemplary leadership, laid a foundation that endures in every Christian community that stands upon the New Testament witness.

4.1.4 Tensions and Triumphs

While the apostles' words carried divine authority, their ministry also sparked significant resistance. Acts 4:1–22 details how Peter and John were arrested by the Sanhedrin, who commanded them to stop preaching about Jesus. Rather than cower, they asserted their higher obedience to God, proclaiming that salvation is found in no one else (Acts 4:19–20). Such conflicts underlined a dynamic tension: the apostolic oracle was unstoppable because it was rooted not in human power, but in the unshakeable commission from Christ.

Despite persecutions, imprisonments, and even martyrdom (e.g., James in Acts 12:1–2), the apostolic message spread. By the time we conclude the Book of Acts, the Gospel has reached Rome—essentially the center of the known world—through the ministry of Paul and his companions. This expansion testifies to the divine impetus behind the apostolic oracle. Human opposition, cultural differences, and logistical challenges could not thwart the unfolding of God's redemptive plan, a reality that underscores the unstoppable force of truth when proclaimed in the power of the Holy Spirit.

4.2 Paul's Epistles as Prophetic Wisdom

4.2.1 Paul's Unique Calling and Apostolic Authority

Among the apostolic voices, Paul's stands out for both its prolific nature—thirteen letters in the New Testament bear his name—and its distinctive emphasis on the mystery of Christ. Formerly a zealous Pharisee and persecutor of the church (Galatians 1:13–14; Acts 9:1–2), Paul encountered the risen Jesus on the road to Damascus (Acts 9:3–9). This dramatic reversal set the stage for Paul's apostleship to the Gentiles, a calling he embraces wholeheartedly (Romans 1:1; Galatians 1:15–16).

Paul's apostolic claim was challenged at times by others who disputed his credentials (2 Corinthians 11:5; Galatians 1:11–12). Yet he consistently defended his apostleship by pointing to three realities: (1) his direct commission from the risen Christ, (2) the fruit of his ministry among Gentiles, and (3) the supernatural revelations that unveiled deep spiritual truths to him (2 Corinthians 12:1–4). Far from seeking personal gain, Paul often ministered under extreme hardship and made "tentmaking" his trade so as not to burden new converts financially (Acts 18:3; 1 Corinthians 9:12, 15). His willingness to suffer—imprisonment, beatings, shipwrecks—demonstrates the seriousness with which he viewed his divine calling and the unstoppable nature of God's oracle through him.

4.2.2 The Concept of "Mystery" in Paul's Writings

Paul frequently employs the Greek term *mystērion* to describe aspects of God's plan that were concealed in ages past but have now come to light in Christ. For Paul, *mystery* is not an esoteric secret known only to a spiritual elite; rather, it is a grace-filled disclosure made possible by God's initiative.

- **Ephesians 3:4–6**: Paul states that "the mystery of Christ" is that Gentiles are co-heirs with Jews, forming one unified body in Him. This revelation shatters centuries of religious and cultural barriers, displaying the expansive scope of God's redemptive work.

- **Colossians 1:26–27**: Here, Paul speaks of "the mystery hidden for ages and generations but now revealed to his saints," which is "Christ in you, the hope of glory." The indwelling presence of Christ in every believer—Jew or Gentile—constitutes the profound secret that even angelic beings marveled over (1 Peter 1:12).
- **Romans 16:25–27**: In his doxology, Paul praises God for "the revelation of the mystery hidden for long ages past." He underscores that this once-hidden plan is now openly proclaimed for all nations to come to the obedience of faith.

These references to mystery underscore how Paul viewed himself as a steward of a newly unveiled divine oracle. Where Old Testament prophets often foresaw the Messiah's coming through types and shadows, Paul, on the other side of the Cross and Pentecost, could elucidate the fullness of God's redemptive strategy. This revelation included not only justification by faith in Christ (Romans 3:21–26) but also the radical unity of believers across ethnic and social lines (Galatians 3:28; Ephesians 2:11–22).

4.2.3 Themes of Paul's Apostolic Oracles

Scattered throughout Paul's letters are recurring theological and practical threads that function much like "apostolic oracles" for the nascent Christian communities. Some of the most prominent include:

1. **Justification by Faith**: Perhaps best illustrated in Romans and Galatians, this doctrine states that human beings are counted righteous before God not by works of the law but through faith in Jesus Christ. This teaching clarified centuries of confusion about how to achieve right standing with God, highlighting grace as the bedrock of salvation (Galatians 2:16; Romans 5:1–2).

2. **Union with Christ**: For Paul, being "in Christ" is more than a theological concept; it is the essence of Christian identity. Believers participate in Christ's death, burial, and resurrection (Romans 6:3–6; Colossians 2:12), enabling them to live in the power of the Spirit (Romans 8:9–11).
3. **Sanctification and Ethical Instructions**: The moral vision Paul imparts is profoundly shaped by the indwelling of the Holy Spirit. Passages like Galatians 5:16–26 contrast life in the flesh with life in the Spirit, urging believers to cultivate virtues such as love, joy, and peace. In Ephesians 4–5, Paul offers guidelines for interpersonal relationships, community unity, and marriage, all framed by the overarching principle of mutual submission and sacrificial love.
4. **Eschatological Hope**: Paul looks forward to the resurrection of the dead and the restoration of all things under Christ (1 Corinthians 15; Romans 8:18–25). This eschatological perspective imbues believers with a hope that transcends current suffering, reminding them that their ultimate destiny is participation in God's eternal kingdom.

Each of these themes can be understood as an extension of Paul's divine mandate to reveal "the mysteries" of the Christian faith. His writings, therefore, remain a treasure trove of divine oracles, offering guidance, reproof, exhortation, and comfort to believers of every generation.

4.2.4 The Pastoral Heart of Apostolic Ministry

While Paul often wrote profound theological treatises, his letters also show a tender pastoral concern. In 1 Thessalonians 2:7–12, he describes himself as both a mother caring for her children and a father urging them to walk in a manner worthy of God. The warmth and affection evident in Philippians 1:3–8, where he expresses deep gratitude and longing for the believers in Philippi, illustrates that apostolic authority was exercised in a relational, nurturing manner, rather than through mere dictates from above.

Paul's dealings with the Corinthian church further exemplify this pastoral dimension. Confronting divisions, immorality, and misunderstandings about spiritual gifts, Paul does not merely condemn wrongdoing; he diagnoses the root causes and points the community back to the centrality of love and unity in the Spirit (1 Corinthians 13–14). This shepherding quality underscores that the apostolic oracle was never intended to be detached from the lived realities of the faith community. Rather, it was woven into the very fabric of the Church's daily struggles, joys, and aspirations.

4.2.5 Contending for the Faith

In defending the truth of the apostolic message against various distortions, Paul shows remarkable intellectual rigor and passion. Galatians stands out as a vigorous polemic against Judaizers who insisted Gentile converts must adhere to circumcision and the Mosaic Law to be saved. Paul's response is unequivocal: adding legal observances as a requirement for justification effectively nullifies the sufficiency of Christ's sacrifice (Galatians 2:21; 5:1–12).

Similarly, in Colossians, Paul confronts syncretistic teachings that combined elements of Jewish legalism, pagan philosophy, and mysticism. His rebuttal centers on the supremacy and sufficiency of Christ: "For in him the whole fullness of deity dwells bodily" (Colossians 2:9). These conflicts reveal that apostolic ministry involved not only proclaiming mysteries but also preserving them from heretical distortions. By engaging in doctrinal correction and establishing guardrails, Paul and his fellow apostles safeguarded the purity of the faith, ensuring the church would remain anchored in the unchangeable truth of the Gospel.

4.3 John's Revelation – The Final Oracle

4.3.1 The Apostle John's Distinctive Voice

The New Testament canon culminates with the Book of Revelation, attributed to the Apostle John. Church tradition holds that John wrote this apocalyptic text while in exile on the island of Patmos (Revelation 1:9). By this stage in his life, John had witnessed both the explosive growth of the Church and fierce waves of persecution under Roman rule. He had also, according to tradition, outlived most of the other apostles, leaving him in a unique position to deliver a final, climactic oracle that addressed both the present challenges and ultimate destiny of God's people.

While John's Gospel and Epistles emphasize themes of love, light, and life, Revelation unveils a grand cosmic drama in which the Lamb triumphs over the forces of evil. Its vivid symbolism—visions of heavenly thrones, fearsome beasts, and bowls of wrath—portrays ultimate realities behind the veil of human history. In many ways, Revelation both builds upon and transcends earlier apostolic writings, casting the final spotlight on Christ as the exalted King who will soon return to fully establish His kingdom.

4.3.2 Understanding the Apocalyptic Genre

Revelation belongs to the literary genre of "apocalyptic," which frequently uses symbolic imagery to convey spiritual truths and future events. Old Testament books like Daniel and Zechariah pave the way for such visionary expressions. Yet John's Revelation stands apart in its comprehensive portrayal of eschatological (end-times) events, linking the spiritual battles of the present age with the climactic showdown at history's close.

One hallmark of apocalyptic literature is the presence of angelic guides, sealed scrolls, and cosmic conflicts that depict the broader struggle between good and evil. John's Revelation employs these motifs to highlight the sovereignty of God over all creation. Even when earthly powers appear dominant, the reader is assured that Christ ultimately holds the keys of history—an assurance that provided hope to early Christians threatened by imperial might.

4.3.3 The Seven Churches as Contemporary Oracles

Before revealing the sweeping eschatological visions, John first delivers specific messages to seven local churches in Asia Minor (Revelation 2–3). These letters reflect Christ's intimate knowledge of each congregation's spiritual condition—praising virtues, rebuking compromises, and calling for repentance where necessary.

1. **Ephesus (Revelation 2:1–7)**: Commended for its perseverance and rejection of false apostles, yet reprimanded for losing its "first love."
2. **Smyrna (Revelation 2:8–11)**: Encouraged to remain faithful amidst persecution, with no reproof given.
3. **Pergamum (Revelation 2:12–17)**: Warned about tolerating false teaching, specifically the "teaching of Balaam."
4. **Thyatira (Revelation 2:18–29)**: Praised for love and service but admonished for tolerating the "woman Jezebel."
5. **Sardis (Revelation 3:1–6)**: Called to wake up and strengthen what remains, having a reputation of being alive yet spiritually dead.
6. **Philadelphia (Revelation 3:7–13)**: Commended for steadfast faith, encouraged with the promise of an open door.
7. **Laodicea (Revelation 3:14–22)**: Infamous for being lukewarm, neither hot nor cold, and exhorted to repent and seek true spiritual riches.

These letters illustrate the pastoral and prophetic thrust of John's Revelation. Before unveiling cosmic judgments, Christ addresses tangible realities within local congregations. This pattern reiterates a core principle of biblical revelation: divine truth speaks directly to real-life contexts, calling believers to practical obedience and holiness. Even the most exalted end-time oracles include moral imperatives for the present.

4.3.4 Apocalyptic Imagery and Themes

Following the messages to the seven churches, John's vision shifts dramatically to the heavenly throne room (Revelation 4–5). Here, he beholds a scroll sealed with seven seals, which only the Lamb—identified as the "Lion of the tribe of Judah" (Revelation 5:5–6)—is worthy to open. This moment underscores a foundational theology: Christ, through His sacrificial death and resurrection, holds the authority to enact God's ultimate plan for history.

From Revelation 6 onward, the narrative unfolds a series of judgments—seals, trumpets, and bowls—that affect both the natural world and rebellious humanity. Though fearsome in scope, these judgments are consistently framed as righteous responses to persistent sin and the oppression of God's people. Interspersed throughout are visions of cosmic warfare (Revelation 12–13), a false prophet, and a "beast" that wields great power on the earth—commonly interpreted as representations of demonic influence and tyrannical governments.

Beneath the harrowing imagery lie crucial theological motifs:

1. **God's Sovereignty**: Despite the apparent chaos, every action unfolds under God's sovereign directive. Angels carry out judgments only when commanded, and Satan's powers remain constrained by divine permission (Revelation 9:1–5).
2. **The Vindication of the Saints**: Those who remain faithful to Christ, even unto death, are promised vindication and reward. Revelation 7:9–17 offers a vision of a vast multitude from every nation, standing before the throne in white robes, signifying victory through the Lamb's blood.
3. **The Ultimate Defeat of Evil**: Revelation 19–20 depicts Christ's triumphant return, the defeat of the beast and false prophet, and eventually, the final casting of Satan into the lake of fire (Revelation 20:10). These events symbolize the end of the rebellion that

began in Eden and affirm that evil does not have the last word.

4.3.5 The Consummation: New Heavens and New Earth

The climax of Revelation—and indeed the entire biblical narrative—arrives in Chapters 21 and 22, where John witnesses the descent of the New Jerusalem. This city, radiant like a bride, represents the perfect union of God and His people, free from pain, mourning, or death (Revelation 21:4). The imagery here starkly contrasts with the fallen cities described earlier in the text, underscoring a complete reversal of the curse introduced in Genesis 3.

In this new creation, there is no temple structure (Revelation 21:22), for the Lord God Almighty and the Lamb are its temple. The distinction between sacred and secular disappears when God's direct presence illuminates everything. The Tree of Life reappears, yielding fruit for the healing of the nations (Revelation 22:2), suggesting that paradise lost in Eden is now eternally restored.

This sweeping portrayal of final redemption is the ultimate apostolic oracle—a grand theological tapestry that binds together the threads of promise, prophecy, and fulfillment laid out through all previous scriptures. John's Revelation hence serves as a triumphant coda to the apostolic age, revealing not merely future events but the heart of God's eternal plan: to reconcile and dwell with His people forever (Ephesians 1:9–10).

In conclusion, within the New Testament witness, the apostles emerge as uniquely commissioned "oracles" who unveil the grandeur of God's redemptive plan through word and deed. Their message bridges the era inaugurated by Jesus—whom they encountered directly—and the subsequent generations who have embraced the Gospel purely on the basis of the apostolic testimony. Whether through Peter's preaching in Jerusalem, Paul's letters to fledgling Gentile congregations, or John's apocalyptic vision on Patmos, each apostolic voice contributes vital contours to the Church's understanding of the "mysteries" once hidden but now revealed.

1. **Apostolic Foundation for the Church**: In Acts, the apostles laid the groundwork for a global movement centered upon the risen Christ. Their Spirit-empowered preaching transcended ethnic barriers, turning hearts toward repentance and forging communities characterized by unity, generosity, and worship.

2. **Paul's Role in Unveiling the Mystery**: As the apostle to the Gentiles, Paul developed profound theological insights into salvation, sanctification, and the believer's union with Christ. His letters, borne out of pastoral concern and doctrinal precision, navigate issues ranging from church discipline to eschatological hope, offering "oracles" that remain instructive for every generation of believers.

3. **John's Revelation as the Culminating Oracle**: The Book of Revelation presents a cosmic panorama of final judgment and eternal restoration. Positioned at the close of the New Testament canon, it completes the apostolic message by affirming Christ's ultimate victory over evil and the establishment of a new heavens and new earth.

Together, these apostles function as a chorus of voices, each adding distinct harmonies yet unified by a single divine melody: the lordship of Christ, the sufficiency of His atoning work, and the Spirit's transformative power at work in His Church. They do not merely recount historical facts or offer speculative theology; they speak with the conviction of those entrusted with a living, God-breathed oracle.

For contemporary believers, the apostolic writings are far more than relics of an ancient faith. They serve as a perpetual standard by which we measure doctrine, moral conduct, and ecclesial practice. Through their inspired words, the Holy Spirit continues to address the Church, reminding us that we stand in continuity with the same redemptive narrative begun among a small band of disciples in first-century Palestine. These oracles remain as urgent and relevant now as when they were first penned, guiding us into the mysteries of grace and urging us to remain steadfast until the consummation revealed in the final pages of Revelation.

In this sense, the apostolic oracle is not locked in the past; it is a living voice that still challenges, comforts, and calls. It beckons each new generation to embrace the mystery of "Christ in you, the hope of glory" (Colossians 1:27), to contend for the faith once delivered to the saints (Jude 3), and to keep our eyes on the promise of Christ's glorious return (2 Peter 3:12–13). As we heed the apostolic word, we find ourselves participating in the very story they proclaimed—a story that extends beyond time into the unending fellowship of Father, Son, and Holy Spirit.

Chapter 5: The Written Word – Scripture as Oracle

Throughout history, religious communities have preserved sacred writings they believed to be divinely inspired. These writings collectively form what Christians refer to as the Old Testament and New Testament—together, "the Bible." For believers, the Bible is more than an ancient book or a collection of spiritual insights; it is the **Word of God**, carrying prophetic, instructive, and transformative power. When people speak of Scripture as an "oracle," they emphasize that this text is not merely human reflection on the divine, but an actual communication from God to humanity, preserved across centuries to guide, correct, encourage, and reveal truth.

The significance of Scripture in Christian life cannot be overstated. Church history is replete with testimonies of those who found in the Bible a living, active voice that addressed their deepest fears, clarified moral quandaries, and fueled spiritual renewal. While God certainly can and does speak in myriad ways, the formation and transmission of the biblical canon give unique weight to this written Word—treated as an enduring standard of doctrine and practice. This chapter explores the historical process by which Scripture was recognized, the theological foundations supporting its divine inspiration and authority, and the practical importance of engaging with God's written Word as the abiding "oracle."

5.1 The Canon of Scripture

5.1.1 Defining "Canon"

The term "canon" (from the Greek kanōn, meaning "measuring rod" or "standard") refers to the collection of books that the Church universally accepts as authoritative Scripture. While Christians agree broadly on the sixty-six books that constitute the Old and New Testaments, historical nuances exist concerning the timing, criteria, and discussions that led to the confirmation of these canonical texts. Nevertheless, the essential concept of a "canon" is that there is a specific, recognized body of writings through which God has chosen to communicate with His people in a uniquely authoritative and enduring manner.

The Old Testament canon, inherited from the Jewish community, contains thirty-nine books (in most Protestant Christian enumerations) that chart the history of Israel, reveal the Law, and contain prophetic and wisdom literature. The New Testament canon, established in the wake of Christ's earthly ministry and the apostolic age, includes twenty-seven books detailing the life of Jesus, the spread of the early Church, various epistles (letters) to Christian communities, and a final apocalyptic revelation. Together, these writings form the complete Christian Bible, a cohesive narrative of redemption that begins with creation and culminates in the promise of a new heavens and new earth.

5.1.2 Formation of the Old Testament Canon

Long before the birth of Jesus, Jewish communities revered a set of writings they believed to be given by God. The Torah (the first five books, often called the Pentateuch) held prime status as it outlined the Law, recounting the creation narrative, the patriarchal history, and Israel's formation as a nation under the covenant with Yahweh. The remaining books—Prophets and Writings—were added as they were recognized to bear divine authority. Prophetic voices, such as Isaiah or Jeremiah, were canonized based on their historical reliability, alignment with prior revelation about God's character, and the confirmation that these texts indeed carried God's authoritative word. Likewise, wisdom books like Psalms, Proverbs, and Ecclesiastes found acceptance due to their alignment with the covenant framework and their consistent portrayal of God's righteousness and human moral responsibility.

By the time of the first century AD, Jewish communities had broadly recognized these texts as sacred, though minor regional variations in ordering or grouping existed. The concept of a "closed" canon for the Hebrew Scriptures became more firmly established in the decades following the destruction of the Second Temple (AD 70). Jesus Himself referenced these writings (often summarized as "the Law and the Prophets," e.g., Matthew 5:17) as bearing divine witness— an indication that the Scriptures already carried a canonical weight among first-century Jews.

5.1.3 Formation of the New Testament Canon

In the New Testament era, the Church discerned the authoritative nature of apostolic writings over the course of several centuries. The Gospels—Matthew, Mark, Luke, and John—took precedence as testimonies of Jesus' life, teachings, death, and resurrection. Because of their close linkage to either direct apostolic witness or reliable apostolic companions, these four were almost universally embraced by early Christians, effectively overshadowing other purported "gospels" with questionable origins or divergent theology.

The Book of Acts, attributed to Luke, offered a historically grounded continuation of the Gospel narrative, detailing the spread of Christianity through the Apostles' ministry. Paul's epistles, written to various churches (Romans, Corinthians, Galatians, and so on) and individuals (Timothy, Titus, Philemon), gained quick recognition because of Paul's unique apostolic calling and the profound impact his writings had on shaping orthodox Christian belief. Letters from other apostolic figures—like James, Peter, John, and Jude—were similarly esteemed for their direct link to the earliest witness of the resurrected Christ.

By the second and third centuries, Church leaders began compiling lists of recognized sacred writings. Notable among these is the Muratorian Fragment (late second century), which affirms most New Testament texts, and Eusebius of Caesarea's fourth-century discussion on widely accepted and disputed books. The councils of Hippo (AD 393) and Carthage (AD 397) marked milestones in publicly listing the twenty-seven New Testament books as canonical, though the practical acceptance of these texts had been widespread for generations. Despite variations in how certain local churches approached books like Revelation or Hebrews, the consensus that ultimately emerged was that these writings bore unique apostolic authority and consistent teaching with the "rule of faith" affirmed in the early Church.

5.1.4 Criteria for Canonicity

While the exact processes were complex and sometimes messy, a few criteria commonly emerge in discussions about how and why certain texts were recognized as canonical:

1. **Apostolic Origins or Connection**: Texts were favored that were authored by an apostle (e.g., Paul, Peter) or a close associate (e.g., Mark's connection to Peter, Luke's association with Paul).
2. **Orthodox Teaching**: Any writing that contradicted the essential doctrines passed down from the apostles was dismissed. The "rule of faith" acted like a doctrinal yardstick to measure consistency with the teachings of Christ and the apostles.
3. **Widespread Usage in Worship**: Books that were consistently used and read in local congregations across various regions carried added weight. The Church recognized the Holy Spirit's guidance in the consistent edification these texts provided.

4. **Internal Witness of the Spirit**: Although more subjective, early believers testified to the Spirit's confirming work in their hearts, affirming these writings as truly God-breathed. This communal discernment was crucial, reflecting Jesus' promise that the Spirit would guide His followers "into all truth" (John 16:13).

These criteria underscore that canonicity was not arbitrarily assigned by a small group but recognized collectively by the believing community over time. The Church did not "create" Scripture; rather, it recognized in certain writings the unmistakable stamp of divine inspiration and authority.

5.1.5 The Canon as a Unified Story

The sixty-six books of the Bible, while diverse in genre, authorship, and historical context, weave together a single overarching narrative. From Genesis to Revelation, a coherent storyline emerges: creation, fall, covenant, redemption, and consummation. The final chapters of the Bible echo the initial chapters of Genesis—revealing a new creation where sin and death no longer hold sway, and God's people dwell eternally in His presence (Revelation 21–22).

This grand narrative offers a Christ-centered focus. While the Old Testament lays the groundwork with prophecies, typologies, and covenants that anticipate a coming Messiah, the New Testament reveals Jesus as that Messiah and expands on the implications for both Jew and Gentile. Thus, one of the reasons the biblical canon resonates so powerfully is its thematic unity, pointing to one God, one plan of redemption, and a single culminating hope for humanity.

5.2 Inspiration and Authority of the Word

5.2.1 Understanding "God-Breathed" Scripture

Central to viewing the Bible as an oracle is the conviction that its writings are **divinely inspired**—that is, the Holy Spirit superintended the writing process to communicate God's will without error in its God-intended message. The classic text underscoring this belief is 2 Timothy 3:16, which states, "All Scripture is breathed out by God..." (ESV). The Greek term translated "breathed out" (*theopneustos*) conveys a profound theological reality: the written Word originates from God's creative breath.

This concept does not imply that human authors were in a trance or that their personalities vanished. Rather, the Spirit worked through their individual vocabularies, cultural backgrounds, and experiences, ensuring the result accurately conveyed divine truth. The synergy of the human and the divine in Scripture is akin to the Incarnation, where Jesus was fully God and fully man—an intricate blending of the supernatural with the natural. Consequently, while many ancient texts can claim historical or literary significance, the Bible stands uniquely as a text that reveals God's counsel in a manner that surpasses ordinary human authorship.

5.2.2 Varieties of Inspiration Theories

Over the centuries, theologians have wrestled with explaining how inspiration works. Several models or theories have emerged:

1. **Verbal Plenary Inspiration**: Asserts that the Holy Spirit superintended every word, not merely the general ideas or themes. Proponents of this view maintain that, because the Scripture's authority rests in God's authorship, each word carries significance—though still conditioned by the original languages and contexts.
2. **Dynamic or Limited Inspiration**: Suggests that God inspired the overarching ideas or theological messages, but that cultural and scientific details might reflect the limitations of the human authors' contexts. Critics of this view caution that it can lead to subjective "picking and choosing" of which parts are genuinely God's Word.
3. **Illumination Theory**: Emphasizes the Holy Spirit's role in illuminating the minds of authors rather than dictating words. This approach underscores the

continuity between the inspiration of biblical authors and the Spirit's ongoing work in believers, though it can blur the distinction between canonical Scripture and other Spirit-led writings.

While Christian traditions may vary in nuance, most converge on the belief that the final text, as recognized in the canon, is entirely trustworthy and authoritative for faith and practice. The degree to which every detail is inerrant or infallible might be debated, but the shared foundation is that Scripture, in its intended purpose, reflects God's wisdom and therefore commands reverence, obedience, and careful study.

5.2.3 Biblical Authority in Church History

From the early centuries of the Church, councils and theologians upheld Scripture's supreme authority in matters of doctrine and ethics. When controversies arose—be they Christological debates about Jesus' nature or disputes about salvation's dynamics—leaders turned to Scripture as the final arbiter of truth. St. Augustine famously wrote, "When the Bible speaks, God speaks," encapsulating the widespread reverence for the text.

The Protestant Reformation (16th century) intensified this focus under the principle of **sola Scriptura** ("Scripture alone"). Reformers like Martin Luther and John Calvin argued that ultimate authority in the Church does not reside in ecclesiastical traditions or papal decrees but in the written Word of God. This emphasis led to translations of the Bible into vernacular languages, facilitating direct access for laypeople. Even in traditions that also esteem Church teachings and apostolic tradition, Scripture remains the foundational norm that guides and measures all other forms of instruction or tradition.

5.2.4 Scripture's Role in Shaping Doctrine and Ethics

Accepting the Bible as God's inspired Word has profound implications for theology and moral guidance. Doctrinally, Christians derive core truths—such as the Triune nature of

God, the sacrificial death and resurrection of Christ, and the promise of salvation by grace through faith—directly from biblical revelation. Ethical stances on issues like marriage, sexuality, economic justice, and neighborly love are likewise grounded in biblical teachings.

Passages like Psalm 119:105 ("Your word is a lamp to my feet and a light to my path") and Matthew 7:24–27 (the parable of building on the rock) illustrate that reliance on Scripture not only informs but transforms believers. Being "doers of the word, and not hearers only" (James 1:22) underscores that biblical authority is not merely theoretical; it demands practical obedience. Believers look to Scripture for principles to shape their daily decisions—how they spend money, how they engage in relationships, and how they respond to societal injustices. Thus, Scripture's authority stands as both a beacon of truth and a moral compass directing faithful living.

5.2.5 Addressing Common Objections

Critics question the Bible's reliability for various reasons, such as perceived contradictions, the presence of supernatural events, or the historical context of its composition. In response, many Christian apologists and scholars highlight the remarkable archaeological corroborations of biblical narratives, the consistency of core doctrinal affirmations across different authors, and the self-authenticating nature of Scripture when read in faith.

- **Apparent Contradictions**: Detailed study often reveals that supposed discrepancies stem from differences in perspective, literary style, or cultural idioms.
- **Miraculous Content**: For those who accept God's existence and sovereignty, miracles become coherent within the biblical worldview, which proclaims that God regularly interacts with creation.
- **Historical Context**: Rather than diminish Scripture's authority, an awareness of cultural and historical settings can deepen our appreciation for how God uniquely spoke into real-world situations.

No text spanning multiple authors, cultures, and centuries can be read simplistically. Yet countless believers assert that deeper engagement with Scripture Intensifies rather than undermines confidence in its divine origin and life-changing power.

5.3 The Bible in the Believer's Life

5.3.1 Hearing God Through Scripture

If Scripture is indeed God's oracle—the abiding, written expression of His will—then reading, studying, and meditating upon it becomes a primary avenue for encountering His voice. Passages like Hebrews 4:12 describe the Word as "living and active, sharper than any two-edged sword," indicating its power to pierce hearts and reveal intentions. In daily practice, believers often find that specific verses speak to their immediate life situations with uncanny relevance—a phenomenon attributed to the Holy Spirit's work in applying Scripture personally.

In corporate worship, the public reading and exposition of Scripture have historically been central. Sermons rooted in biblical texts allow congregations to hear God's message collectively, fostering unity in understanding and application. Meanwhile, personal devotional habits—ranging from systematic Bible reading plans to lectio divina (a contemplative approach of slowly meditating on short passages)—provide intimate moments of divine encounter. Through these practices, Scripture becomes the living oracle, bridging the centuries to address hearts here and now.

5.3.2 Spiritual Formation and Discipleship

Engaging with the Bible shapes a believer's inner life, fostering spiritual maturity. The Psalmist in Psalm 1:2-3 likens the person who meditates on God's law to a tree planted by streams of water, yielding fruit in season. Such imagery underscores the sustaining effect of Scripture on spiritual vitality.

- **Renewing the Mind**: Romans 12:2 exhorts believers not to conform to the world but to be transformed by the renewing of their minds. Immersing oneself in biblical truths recalibrates thought patterns, values, and motivations.
- **Guiding Moral Decisions**: Ethical dilemmas, whether personal or communal, find clarity when weighed against scriptural principles. When faced with decisions about honesty, purity, or generosity, believers often ask, "What does Scripture say?"
- **Encouraging Prayerful Reflection**: As believers read Scripture, they frequently respond with prayer, turning biblical promises or convictions into petitions, praises, or confessions. This dialogue fosters a deeper relational engagement with God.

Beyond individual transformation, Scripture-based discipleship involves teaching newer believers how to interpret and apply Scripture faithfully. Mentoring relationships can focus on shared Bible reading, promoting accountability and deeper understanding. In many traditions, small groups or Sunday schools systematically walk through entire books of the Bible, thereby equipping members to handle the Word responsibly and fruitfully.

5.3.3 Community and the Shared Interpretation of Scripture

While personal reading is invaluable, Christianity is inherently communal. The New Testament epistles were originally addressed to congregations, anticipating that believers would hear and discuss them together. This communal context acts as a safeguard against purely subjective or idiosyncratic interpretations. As believers gather to study, they test one another's insights, refine their understanding, and correct misunderstandings. Church history, creeds, and commentaries also provide checks and balances, reminding readers that their engagement with Scripture does not occur in a vacuum.

Moreover, local churches often incorporate formal confession of faith or doctrinal statements grounded in Scripture, reinforcing unity. Though interpretational diversity can exist—hence the existence of various denominations—most orthodox traditions agree on fundamental doctrines (e.g., the deity of Christ, salvation by grace through faith) precisely because these are solidly attested in Scripture. The communal interplay between Scripture, tradition, and the Holy Spirit's guidance fosters a balanced approach to reading the biblical oracle.

5.3.4 Overcoming Challenges in Biblical Engagement

For many believers, the Bible can appear intimidating. Its breadth, cultural distance, ancient languages, and varied genres can present obstacles. Yet Scripture itself exhorts diligence in study: "Study to show yourself approved unto God, a worker who does not need to be ashamed, rightly handling the word of truth" (2 Timothy 2:15). Several strategies help overcome these challenges:

1. **Reading Plans and Study Tools**: Organized plans (e.g., "read the Bible in a year") help believers engage systematically. Study Bibles, concordances, and commentaries provide historical and linguistic context, making difficult passages clearer.
2. **Pastoral and Teaching Ministries**: Well-trained pastors, teachers, and small group leaders help interpret passages accurately, bridging cultural and historical gaps. Workshops, seminars, or Bible training courses can bolster believers' confidence in handling Scripture.
3. **The Role of the Holy Spirit**: According to John 16:13, the Spirit guides believers into truth. Many testify that prayerful reliance on the Spirit transforms the reading experience, turning seemingly opaque texts into revelations of God's wisdom.

Despite difficulties, persevering in biblical engagement yields profound rewards. Over time, believers witness Scripture shaping their worldview, moral compass, and relationship with God and others in ways no other text can replicate.

5.3.5 Practical Application and Transformation

The Bible's authority and message aim for transformation, not mere information transfer. James 1:22–25 warns against being hearers only, likening such a person to someone who looks in a mirror and forgets their reflection. Genuine interaction with Scripture calls for obedient response: repenting of identified sins, practicing newly revealed virtues, and allowing God to reorder one's priorities.

- **Personal Holiness**: Passages such as 1 Peter 1:15–16 call believers to be holy as God is holy. Engaging with Scripture exposes both areas of sin and strategies for growth, emphasizing grace and the Spirit's empowerment.
- **Social and Cultural Engagement**: Many biblical imperatives relate to justice, compassion, and mercy, inspiring believers to serve the marginalized, advocate for ethical policies, and embody the love of Christ in the public sphere.
- **Evangelism and Apologetics**: Knowledge of Scripture equips believers to share the Gospel more persuasively and answer skeptics respectfully (1 Peter 3:15). Familiarity with key passages and the overarching biblical narrative can turn everyday conversations into opportunities for testimony.

Ultimately, Scripture's transformative power rests in its divine origin. Because it is "living and abiding" (1 Peter 1:23), it encounters readers at the deepest levels of belief and identity, compelling them to grow ever closer to God's likeness.

In conclusion, this chapter is a foundational dimension of the Christian faith: that God, who spoke through prophets and ultimately through His Son, has also seen fit to preserve His message in written form, accessible to every generation. Far from being a static repository of religious traditions, the Bible is alive with divine breath, brimming with historical narratives that shape our understanding of God's redemptive acts, moral directives that cut through cultural relativism, and a grand eschatological hope that anchors our present struggles.

1. **The Canon as a Providential Legacy**: The Bible did not emerge haphazardly. Through centuries of faithful transmission and communal discernment, the Church recognized a set of writings whose unity and authority transcend human authorship. This canon now stands as a testament to God's sovereign guidance in human history, ensuring believers today can open its pages and hear the same truths that animated the faith of saints across millennia.

2. **Inspiration and Authority**: Scriptural inspiration rests on the conviction that God's Spirit guided each author, safeguarding the message from error in its divine purpose. Because the Bible carries God's imprimatur, it holds supreme authority for shaping Christian doctrine and ethics, speaking to issues both timeless and contemporary.

3. **Practical Engagement for Transformation**: Engaging with Scripture cannot remain a purely intellectual pursuit; it calls for prayerful reflection, communal dialogue, and life application. As believers heed the Bible's words, they find guidance for moral dilemmas, comfort in affliction, and a potent impetus for social justice. In short, the Word of God molds hearts to reflect His character.

4. **Eternal Resonance**: Jesus declared, "Heaven and earth will pass away, but my words will not pass away" (Matthew 24:35). This promise testifies to the enduring power of Scripture. Even as cultures evolve and new generations wrestle with unprecedented challenges, the Bible's oracles remain relevant, continually addressing the most pressing spiritual, moral, and existential questions.

For readers of this chapter, the invitation is clear: approach Scripture with reverence and expectancy. The same God who spoke creation into existence and sustained His covenant people throughout history still speaks through His written Word. Whether one is new to the faith or a seasoned believer, the Bible offers a divine conversation that refuses to remain locked in antiquity. Under the Spirit's illumination, those sacred pages come alive, testifying that God's voice—His oracle—is as near as the open text before us.

Chapter 6: Modern Echoes – Prophecy in Today's Church

From the prophetic pronouncements of Old Testament figures to the oracles delivered by the apostles in the early Church, believers have long recognized that God can speak in dynamic, revelatory ways. Yet the question remains: does God continue to speak prophetically to His people today, and if so, how should these "modern echoes" be received, tested, and applied?

In many Christian traditions, the idea of God speaking directly—through visions, impressions, words of knowledge, or prophetic utterances—remains both a source of hope and of controversy. Some believers hold that the age of inspired prophecy ended with the close of the apostolic era; others testify to ongoing revelatory experiences that edify the Church and confirm God's active guidance. Whatever one's theological stance, navigating modern claims of prophecy requires biblical discernment, humility, and an understanding that the Spirit of God, if still at work in such ways, will not contradict the essential truths already revealed in Scripture.

This chapter provides an overview of the contemporary landscape of prophecy. We begin with the debate between "continuationist" and "cessationist" perspectives on whether prophetic gifts remain operative. We then explore biblical guidelines for testing modern-day words alleged to come from God, emphasizing spiritual maturity and accountability. Finally, we consider how churches that embrace prophecy seek to integrate this gift into congregational life, so that believers may benefit without falling into misuse or sensationalism.

6.1 The Continuation or Cessation Debate

One of the most significant theological disputes among evangelicals, charismatics, and other Christian denominations centers on whether miraculous gifts—especially prophecy—continue in the post-apostolic age. While Scripture itself underscores the importance of prophecy in the early Church (1 Corinthians 14:1; Acts 2:17–18), various interpreters differ on the timeframe and extent of prophetic manifestations beyond the era of the apostles.

6.1.1 Defining Continuationism

Continuationism holds that all spiritual gifts mentioned in the New Testament, including prophecy, tongues, and healing, remain available to the Church today. Proponents of continuationism assert that there is no clear biblical text indicating these gifts would cease. They often quote 1 Corinthians 13:8–10, pointing out that while prophecy and tongues will eventually cease, that cessation is associated with the arrival of "the perfect," which they interpret as the eschatological consummation of God's kingdom—something that has not yet occurred.

Continuationists also highlight the global and historical testimonies of Christians—both ancient and modern—who claim to have experienced prophetic revelations. They point to spiritual awakenings and revival movements (e.g., among early Methodists, the Azusa Street Revival, the Charismatic

Renewal) where believers reported divine guidance, miraculous healings, or prophetic insights leading to repentance and strengthened faith. Such accounts, in their view, corroborate the biblical promise that the Holy Spirit continues to empower believers for ministry (Acts 1:8; Ephesians 4:11–13).

A key dimension of continuationism is its emphasis on discernment and humility. Continuationists typically affirm the supreme authority of Scripture, insisting that any modern prophecy must align with biblical truth. They see prophecy today as a gift functioning under the guidance of the Holy Spirit, intended for the edification, exhortation, and comfort of the Church (1 Corinthians 14:3). While they acknowledge that false or misguided prophecies can occur, they maintain that the potential for error does not invalidate the gift itself.

6.1.2 Defining Cessationism

Cessationism argues that certain miraculous gifts—particularly prophecy and tongues—were unique to the apostolic era, intended to authenticate the Gospel message before the completion of the New Testament canon. According to this view, once Scripture reached its final form and the Church had been established on the foundation of the apostles, revelatory gifts were no longer necessary. They often invoke Ephesians 2:20, which states the Church is "built on the foundation of the apostles and prophets," implying that, in their interpretation, these foundational roles were confined to the earliest generation of believers.

Cessationists cite historical observations that overtly miraculous or prophetic phenomena seemed less common in certain periods of Church history—though this point is debated, as some Christian traditions preserve reports of miracles throughout the centuries. They also express pastoral concerns, noting that modern claims of prophecy can lead to doctrinal confusion, spiritual abuse, or an overreliance on subjective impressions rather than Scripture. In their understanding, God continues to guide and speak through His written Word and the providential directing of the Holy Spirit, but does not do so through distinct "new prophecies."

Furthermore, cessationists view passages such as Hebrews 1:1–2—where God is said to have spoken definitively through His Son, Jesus Christ—as a theological emphasis that no further revelation is needed beyond what has been recorded in the Bible. While they affirm God's sovereignty and power to perform miracles, they remain cautious about any claim that equates modern "prophetic" utterances with the binding authority of canonical Scripture.

6.1.3 Core Points of Tension

The primary friction between continuationists and cessationists arises from differing interpretations of biblical texts and historical patterns. Both camps agree on the centrality of Christ's redemptive work and the authority of Scripture, yet they arrive at divergent conclusions regarding the nature, frequency, and validity of post-biblical prophecy. Key points include:

1. **Purpose of Prophecy**: Continuationists see ongoing prophecy as part of the Spirit's ministry of building up and guiding the Church, while cessationists believe Scripture alone now fulfills that function authoritatively.
2. **Scriptural Warnings**: Cessationists highlight warnings about false prophets and the sufficiency of written revelation, while continuationists point to equally strong admonitions not to "despise prophecies" but to test them (1 Thessalonians 5:20–21).
3. **Historical Evidence**: Both camps draw on Church history to support their case, noting either the prevalence or absence (as they interpret it) of prophetic activities in different eras.
4. **Practical Outcomes**: Some fear that embracing modern prophecy opens the door to doctrinal chaos, while others argue that quenching the Spirit leads to spiritual stagnation, ignoring legitimate ways God may speak.

Despite these disagreements, many Christians on both sides maintain a respectful dialogue, recognizing each other's commitment to biblical fidelity. A middle ground also exists—some believers hold that prophecy might continue in principle, but exercise caution or claim it is rare. This diversity of perspectives underscores that prophecy remains a nuanced and sometimes controversial topic in the modern Church, inviting ongoing reflection and prayerful study of Scripture.

6.2 Testing Modern-Day Prophecies

Regardless of one's theological stance on prophecy's continuation, the Bible clearly instructs believers to exercise discernment when confronted with any claim of divine revelation. In the Old Testament, false prophets posed a serious threat to Israel's covenant fidelity. Similarly, the New Testament warns that many false prophets and teachers can arise (2 Peter 2:1; 1 John 4:1). Therefore, testing modern-day prophecies is not an optional practice—it is a scriptural mandate that safeguards the Church from deception and spiritual harm.

6.2.1 Biblical Foundations for Discernment

1 Thessalonians 5:20–21 commands believers: "Do not treat prophecies with contempt but test them all; hold on to what is good." This twofold instruction—valuing prophecy yet rigorously testing it—captures the biblical balance. It affirms that genuine prophecy can be a gift from God while acknowledging that not every prophetic claim is trustworthy.

Similarly, 1 John 4:1 admonishes believers to "test the spirits to see whether they are from God," illustrating that not every spiritual utterance or supernatural manifestation originates in divine truth. Such passages anchor discernment in a posture of both openness and caution. We neither automatically reject contemporary claims of prophecy nor accept them blindly.

6.2.2 Criteria for Evaluation

Historically and biblically, Christians have employed several criteria to assess the validity of prophetic words:

1. **Alignment with Scripture** Since the Bible constitutes God's authoritative revelation, any modern prophecy that contradicts scriptural teaching must be rejected. For example, if someone claims a prophetic word that condones theft, adultery, or idolatry, the Church can confidently deem it false based on clear biblical prohibitions (Exodus 20; 1 Corinthians 6:9–10). True prophecy will always reflect the holiness and moral purity revealed in God's Word.

2. **Christological Focus** The Holy Spirit exalts Christ (John 15:26; 16:14). Authentic prophecy will direct attention to Jesus—His lordship, redemption, and glory—rather than magnifying a human prophet or promoting sensationalism. A self-aggrandizing "prophecy" that primarily draws attention to the speaker's spirituality or demands absolute allegiance to a human leader fails the Christ-centered test.

3. **Moral Fruit and Character** Jesus taught that we can recognize false prophets by their fruit (Matthew 7:15–20). While no person is without sin, a consistent pattern of unrepentant immorality, greed, deception, or abuse of authority in the life of a so-called prophet undermines the credibility of their messages. Conversely, those who exhibit humility, servant-heartedness, and alignment with scriptural ethics are more likely to be speaking under genuine inspiration.

4. **Factual Accuracy or Fulfillment (When Applicable)** Deuteronomy 18:22 states that if a prophet's predictions do not come to pass, such a word is not from the Lord. Although some modern prophecies address broader themes of encouragement or guidance rather than specific future events, in cases where predictions are made, consistency with outcomes can be an indicator of authenticity. Caution is advised, however, because timing and interpretation

can be complex; not all prophecies function as straightforward forecasts.
5. **Edification of the Church** 1 Corinthians 14:3 notes that true prophecy in a congregational setting strengthens, encourages, and comforts believers. If a purported prophetic word fosters confusion, discord, or condemnation without leading to repentance or hope, it may not be from the Holy Spirit. Constructive correction can still be edifying if administered in love and guided by God's wisdom.

6.2.3 Pastoral Oversight and Accountability

An additional safeguard involves the role of church leadership and community. The New Testament often envisions prophecy occurring within the context of gathered believers, with others weighing and discerning the message (1 Corinthians 14:29). Spiritual oversight by mature, biblically grounded elders or pastors helps ensure that individual subjective impressions are tested. A community-based approach prevents the isolation or abuse of prophetic gifts by subjecting them to collective wisdom.

Accountability also protects well-intentioned Christians who might mistake personal desires or strong feelings for a divine revelation. Even sincere believers can misinterpret an internal prompting, particularly if they lack experience or biblical grounding. By submitting one's impressions to trusted leaders and peers, potential prophets can receive guidance, correction, or confirmation. This cooperative process fosters humility and helps mitigate the risk of spiritual pride or the potential for harmful manipulations.

6.2.4 Handling Errant Prophecies

If a prophecy proves incorrect, contradictory to Scripture, or spiritually harmful, church leaders must address the situation graciously yet firmly. Depending on the severity of the error, they might offer correction and counsel to the individual who gave the prophecy, emphasizing the need for repentance and deeper discipleship. In extreme cases—particularly where there is willful deception or a refusal to submit to accountability—fellowship restrictions might be necessary to protect the congregation.

Importantly, an errant prophecy does not automatically label someone a "false prophet" in the sense of malicious intention. Many sincere Christians can make mistakes in discerning the voice of God. While false prophets do exist—those who knowingly distort truth for personal gain or lead others astray—misguided believers may simply need instruction, mentorship, and a reminder that prophecy should never overshadow or replace Scripture's authority.

6.3 The Gift of Prophecy in the Body of Christ

In Christian contexts that affirm the ongoing presence of prophetic gifts, there is a desire to integrate such gifts in a way that strengthens the Church without overshadowing the central role of Scripture, the sacraments, and Christ-focused worship. This section explores how believers who embrace modern prophecy can nurture a healthy, biblical practice that edifies the congregation and fosters spiritual growth.

6.3.1 Biblical Vision for Prophetic Ministry

Paul's letters, especially 1 Corinthians 12–14, depict the local assembly as a body composed of many parts, each uniquely endowed with spiritual gifts. Among these gifts, prophecy stands out for its capacity to strengthen believers, bring conviction of sin, and offer timely encouragement (1 Corinthians 14:24–25). Contrary to popular perceptions that equate prophecy only with foretelling events, Paul emphasizes the gift's forth-telling function—delivering messages that illuminate God's heart for a particular moment or need.

In 1 Corinthians 14:1, Paul exhorts believers to "earnestly desire the spiritual gifts, especially that you may prophesy." He qualifies this encouragement, however, by devoting an entire chapter (1 Corinthians 13) to the primacy of love as the essential motivation for all gifts. Love ensures that prophecy does not become a platform for personal pride or divisiveness. Rather, genuine prophecy arises from compassion for God's people and a desire to build them up in faith and obedience.

6.3.2 Congregational Contexts for Prophecy

Churches that welcome prophecy often provide structured opportunities for believers to share words they sense may be from the Lord, while maintaining an orderly and discerning environment:

1. **Designated Times in Worship**: Some congregations set aside a portion of their corporate worship gatherings for brief sharing of words, impressions, or pictures that believers feel prompted to communicate. Leaders may require that all contributions align with biblical truth and be kept succinct. Another leader, such as an elder or pastor, then discerns and comments on these words publicly.
2. **Prophetic Prayer Teams**: Another common format involves small teams dedicated to praying for individuals, listening for the Holy Spirit's guidance, and sharing any insights that emerge. Such teams typically operate under pastoral oversight, ensuring respect, confidentiality, and doctrinal soundness.
3. **Encouragement in Small Groups**: Informal settings—like home-based Bible studies or fellowship groups—can also be conducive to the exercise of prophecy. Participants pray together, sometimes receiving specific encouragement or guidance for one another. Any potentially directive or corrective word is subject to group evaluation, fostering a mutual accountability process.

In each of these contexts, leadership plays a critical role in offering teaching on biblical discernment, setting guidelines to prevent disruptions, and lovingly correcting imbalances. By weaving prophecy into communal rhythms, churches seek to nurture spiritual vitality and sensitivity to the Spirit's leading without veering into sensationalism or neglect of core biblical teaching.

6.3.3 Prophecy and Personal Guidance

A delicate area involves "directive" prophecy—messages that claim to provide specific guidance about personal decisions, such as career moves, marriage partners, or relocation. While Scripture records instances where prophets offered concrete direction (e.g., Agabus warning Paul of imprisonment in Acts 21:10–11), most churches urge caution in delivering or receiving prophecy that dictates personal choices. Several guidelines help maintain wisdom:

- **Submission to Biblical Wisdom**: Any counsel that violates scriptural principles (e.g., endorsing a sinful relationship) can be dismissed outright.
- **Confirmation by the Individual**: Often, a genuine prophetic word about personal matters resonates with what God has already been speaking to a believer's heart. If it comes entirely out of the blue, further prayer, consultation with mature Christians, and patience are recommended before making life-altering decisions.
- **Accountability with Leaders**: Rather than making impulsive changes based on a prophecy, believers are encouraged to share the word with trusted pastors or mentors. If multiple mature believers confirm the direction and biblical alignment, confidence can grow. If there is a caution or check, more time and discernment may be needed.
- **Humility of Delivery**: Those who sense a directive prophecy often present it with humility, clarifying that they could be mistaken. Such caution helps prevent spiritual coercion or undue pressure.

The principle at work is that God can and does guide individuals through various means—Scripture, wise counsel, inner conviction, and occasionally prophetic insight—but each channel is tested and integrated into a larger process of discernment. Genuine revelation from the Spirit will never bypass or diminish a believer's personal relationship with the

Lord, nor will it override the believer's responsibility to seek God's will with scriptural grounding and wise counsel.

6.3.4 Prophecy and Corporate Direction

Beyond personal guidance, some churches have experienced corporate prophetic words that shape ministry initiatives, outreach endeavors, or prayer emphases. For instance, leaders might sense God highlighting a particular unreached neighborhood or pressing social issue. If confirmed through prayer and alignment with the church's vision, these prophetic impressions can spur strategic action and renewed fervor.

Similarly, prophecy can play a role in times of leadership transitions or decision-making processes. Church boards and pastoral teams may invite intercessors or prophetic voices to pray specifically for clarity, believing the Holy Spirit can bring timely confirmation or redirection. However, prudent leaders balance such words with due diligence, organizational planning, and biblical principles of stewardship. If a prophecy claims the church should undertake a massive building project or launch a new campus, for example, the leadership must weigh financial feasibility, unity of vision, and the broader counsel of Scripture (e.g., counting the cost, Luke 14:28) to ensure faith aligns with wisdom.

6.3.5 Guarding Against Abuses and Extremes

Wherever the gift of prophecy is encouraged, potential abuses can arise. Common pitfalls include:

1. **Elevating Prophetic Voices Above Scripture** In some circles, a charismatic leader's prophecies may become functionally more influential than the Bible itself. This scenario is dangerous, for it places human words on par with or above the canonical text, violating principles of biblical authority. Leaders must constantly remind congregations that any human prophecy is subordinate to the written Word.
2. **Creating a Hierarchy of "Super-Spiritual" Believers** If those who prophesy are seen as inherently more

spiritual or closer to God, a subtle elitism can creep in. This dynamic undermines the New Testament teaching that every believer is equally part of the body. 1 Corinthians 12:21–26 emphasizes that each part is indispensable; thus, no single gift or role confers special status.

3. **Manipulation or Control** When "God said…" becomes a tool to coerce compliance with personal agendas, spiritual abuse is at work. Healthy church environments discourage the usage of prophecy for manipulation, encouraging instead a spirit of servanthood and shared discernment.

4. **Over-Reliance on Prophetic Utterances** Even if a church affirms modern prophecy, leaders caution members not to neglect Scripture study, prayer, and practical wisdom. Prophetic words are one tool in God's toolbox; they do not replace consistent Christian discipleship, theological study, or the day-to-day leading of the Holy Spirit in ordinary life.

Addressing these pitfalls requires transparent leadership, ongoing biblical education, and an environment where open questions are welcomed. Some churches hold annual or periodic teachings on prophecy, ensuring new believers receive instruction on discerning, testing, and properly stewarding revelatory gifts. By fostering a humble, Christ-centered culture, congregations can encourage spiritual gifts without falling prey to sensationalism or error.

In conclusion, in this chapter, we grapple with the complex interplay between ancient biblical revelation and the possibility of God's continuing prophetic voice among contemporary believers. The question is not simply whether prophecy is "real" but how it might manifest in a way that honors Scripture, glorifies Christ, and edifies the community of faith. Christians across the theological spectrum can agree that God remains active in His Church and that any purported revelation must be weighed against the unchanging standard of His written Word.

1. **Continuation vs. Cessation**: While some argue that prophetic gifts ceased with the apostles, others maintain that the Spirit still grants visions, impressions, and words of wisdom to guide believers. This debate highlights the diversity within the global Church, prompting both sides to refine their biblical exegesis and historical understanding.
2. **The Mandate to Test**: Regardless of position, Scripture commands testing of alleged revelations. Criteria such as biblical alignment, Christ-centeredness, moral fruit, and factual accuracy help the Church distinguish divine messages from human or deceptive sources. The local body, under wise spiritual leadership, plays a pivotal role in exercising this discernment.
3. **Prophecy in Practical Context**: For those communities that embrace modern prophecy, structured opportunities—whether during worship, in prayer teams, or through small groups—allow believers to share messages in an orderly, accountable environment. Caution and humility, rather than sensational claims or dogmatic certainty, characterize healthy prophetic ministries.
4. **Edification as the Goal**: Whether prophecy reveals an impending crisis or offers gentle encouragement, its ultimate purpose is the upbuilding and sanctification of God's people. By calling individuals and congregations closer to Christ, genuine prophecy fosters repentance, unity, and mission-focused zeal.

In an era when many voices clamor for attention—through social media, politics, and cultural commentary—the Church's challenge is to remain anchored in the timeless truths of Scripture while staying open to the Holy Spirit's living guidance. The legacy of biblical prophecy reminds us that God longs to communicate His heart, correct our course, and instill renewed hope in each generation. Still, any contemporary echo of that prophetic tradition should be measured by the yardstick of God's character and Word.

For those navigating these questions in practical ministry settings, the path forward involves prayer, solid teaching, and a consistent reliance on God's sovereignty. As we humbly seek the Spirit's leading, we can hold prophecy in high regard without idolizing it—recognizing that all revelatory gifts must serve, rather than eclipse, the supreme revelation of God in Jesus Christ and the inspired Scriptures. Such a balanced approach allows modern echoes of prophecy to ring with clarity, resonating with the redemptive melody that has resounded through the Church from its earliest days, and pointing us always back to the One who is the same yesterday, today, and forever (Hebrews 13:8).

Chapter 7: Receiving the Oracle – Hearing God Personally

In the Christian worldview, God is not an impersonal force or a distant deity locked away in heaven. Rather, He is intimately involved with His creation, desiring fellowship with men and women made in His image (Genesis 1:26–27). Throughout Scripture, we see a God who not only initiates covenants and reveals His character but also invites individuals into personal dialogue. From Adam walking with God in the garden (Genesis 3:8) to John hearing the risen Christ's words on the island of Patmos (Revelation 1:9–11), divine-human interaction is portrayed as a living reality rather than a mere theological abstraction.

In contemporary Christian experience, many believers affirm that God still speaks today, not adding new canonical revelation or contradicting Scripture, but guiding, comforting, convicting, and instructing individuals through the Holy Spirit. This personal aspect of hearing God is sometimes referred to as "quiet time," "listening prayer," or the "inner witness" of the Spirit. Yet questions naturally arise: How can one distinguish God's voice from personal thoughts or external influences?

Why do some people seem to hear God clearly while others struggle in confusion or silence? What factors can hinder one's ability to receive the "oracle"—the divine Word—on a personal level?

This chapter aims to address such questions by presenting both biblical foundations and practical steps. It begins by examining the cultivation of a "listening spirit," the posture of heart and practice that opens one to divine communication. Next, it surveys the principal barriers—sin, distraction, and doubt—that can dull spiritual hearing. Finally, it underscores the necessity of obeying God's voice, lest one become a perpetual recipient of revelation without the transformation and fruit that genuine obedience brings. As you read, remember that every believer's journey is unique; the methods and experiences of hearing God vary, but the One who speaks is the same, and His desire is to draw each person deeper into intimate fellowship with Him.

7.1 Cultivating a Listening Spirit

Learning to hear God's voice is not an esoteric practice reserved for mystics or spiritual elites; rather, it is part of the normal Christian life. Jesus Himself stated in John 10:27, "My sheep hear my voice, and I know them, and they follow me." This pastoral imagery conveys a relational dynamic: just as sheep learn to recognize the tone and cadence of their shepherd's call, believers, over time, become attuned to the ways God communicates. Yet this recognition does not occur automatically; it demands intentional cultivation. Below are key elements that foster a "listening spirit."

7.1.1 The Posture of the Heart

A foundational requirement for hearing God is humility. James 4:6 reminds us that "God opposes the proud but gives grace to the humble." Pride blinds us to our dependence on God and can cause us to dismiss the subtle ways He speaks. Conversely, humility opens our hearts to instruction. When we approach God as the source of all wisdom, we position ourselves to learn, to be corrected, and to grow. In practice, this means coming before the Lord daily with a posture of reverence: acknowledging His sovereignty, acknowledging our finite understanding, and inviting Him to speak into our circumstances.

Closely related is the virtue of **expectancy**. Scriptures such as Matthew 7:7–11 invite believers to ask, seek, and knock, promising that a loving Father is eager to respond. A believer who truly expects God to speak is more likely to discern His voice, whether through Scripture, an inner nudge, or a timely word from a fellow Christian. In contrast, cynicism or spiritual apathy stifles receptivity. Cultivating expectancy involves reminding oneself of God's character and faithfulness: if He has spoken throughout biblical history, He is still capable of guiding His children today.

7.1.2 The Discipline of Prayer

While God can speak in myriad ways—through nature, circumstances, or other people—prayer is a unique channel in which two-way communication is deliberately sought. Prayer encompasses praise, thanksgiving, confession, petition, and intercession, yet it can also include listening. Many believers rush through prayer as if it were a one-sided monologue of requests, failing to pause and reflect on how God might respond. Incorporating listening segments within prayer allows room for the Holy Spirit to bring Scripture to mind, impress a direction upon the heart, or illuminate an area of life requiring attention.

Various prayer traditions offer structured methods for developing this listening component. For instance, **lectio divina** (Latin for "divine reading") blends meditative reading of Scripture with quiet reflection and prayerful response, inviting the Word of God to resonate personally. Another approach is "Centering Prayer," which emphasizes silent openness to the presence of God. However, believers need not rely on formal methods alone; simply building a rhythm of pausing in stillness after praying can be sufficient to create space for the Holy Spirit's promptings.

7.1.3 Meditation on Scripture

Because Scripture is God's inspired Word (2 Timothy 3:16), immersing oneself in the Bible is a premier way of learning to recognize His voice. Just as a musician's ear is trained by repeatedly hearing the notes of a scale, the believer's spiritual ear is tuned by exposure to the patterns, values, and truths of God's Word. Through **biblical meditation**, one ponders a passage carefully, perhaps re-reading it slowly, asking questions like: "What does this reveal about God's character? What might the Holy Spirit be highlighting for my life? How can this truth be applied today?"

Meditation differs from simple reading in its contemplative focus. Scriptures such as Psalm 1:2–3 and Joshua 1:8 promise blessing for those who "meditate day and night" on God's laws. This repeated reflection shifts biblical truths from theoretical concepts to lived realities, transforming the reader's mindset and desires. In this climate of internalized Scripture, believers often find that the Holy Spirit personalizes verses for specific life situations. A phrase or command can stand out, providing insight or conviction relevant to a pending decision, a relational conflict, or an emotional struggle.

7.1.4 Fasting and Other Spiritual Disciplines

Fasting—abstaining from food or certain pleasures for a set time—can heighten spiritual sensitivity, according to biblical precedent. Characters such as Moses (Exodus 34:28), Elijah (1 Kings 19:8), and Daniel (Daniel 9:3; 10:2–3) all fasted at pivotal moments, often receiving divine revelation or empowerment afterward. Jesus Himself fasted for forty days in the wilderness (Matthew 4:1–2) before embarking on public ministry, exemplifying how fasting can align the spirit more closely with God's purposes.

While fasting does not coerce God into speaking, it can clarify our spiritual antenna, so to speak, by subduing bodily appetites and distractions. Many contemporary believers testify that during fasts—whether partial or extended—they experience heightened awareness of God's presence and guidance. This practice is best approached prayerfully and responsibly; those with medical conditions, for example, should consult professional advice before attempting prolonged fasts. Nonetheless, fasting remains a biblical tool for cultivating a listening heart and expressing earnestness in seeking the Lord's direction.

Other spiritual disciplines, such as **silence and solitude**, can also nurture attentiveness to God's voice. In an era of constant stimulation—endless notifications, streaming services, and social media—creating intentional times of silence can be challenging yet profoundly rewarding. As Elijah discovered in 1 Kings 19:12–13, God sometimes speaks through a "gentle whisper." Without quiet spaces, that whisper may be drowned out. Retreating periodically to a quiet location, unplugging from digital devices, and simply waiting on God fosters an environment in which the soul can settle, and the Spirit can speak without competing clamor.

7.1.5 Cultivating Community Support

While personal devotion is vital, hearing God is not solely an individualistic endeavor. Healthy spiritual communities encourage one another in the practice of listening. Small groups or prayer partners can share insights gleaned from their devotions, offer feedback on whether a particular impression seems consistent with Scripture, and affirm or gently challenge claims of divine guidance. Mutual encouragement ensures that believers do not isolate themselves with subjective experiences that could become imbalanced.

Moreover, mentors or older believers often provide wisdom grounded in years of experience. Young Christians, eager to hear God, may confuse strong emotions with divine promptings; mentors help them weigh their perceived revelations carefully. In this supportive framework, the fear of "missing God" or "making mistakes" is alleviated by the collective discernment of the body of Christ. As Proverbs 11:14 observes, "in an abundance of counselors there is safety."

7.2 Barriers to Hearing God

Even with sincere intention and faithful practice, many Christians encounter seasons when God's voice seems elusive. Sometimes, these "dry spells" are part of a deeper spiritual training or a call to persevere in faith. In other instances, identifiable barriers—spiritual, emotional, or behavioral—may block one's capacity to receive divine guidance. Understanding and addressing these obstacles can help restore clarity and communion.

7.2.1 The Disruption of Sin

Scripture repeatedly connects sin with a darkening of understanding. Isaiah 59:2, for instance, states, "Your iniquities have made a separation between you and your God, and your sins have hidden his face from you." While the New Testament believer rests in the forgiveness accomplished by Christ, unconfessed or habitual sin can still hinder fellowship with God, clouding spiritual sensitivity. These sins need not be dramatic—pride, resentment, envy, or impurity in thought can accumulate into a hardened heart.

Addressing sin entails genuine repentance and restoration. 1 John 1:9 promises that if we confess our sins, God is faithful to forgive and cleanse us from unrighteousness. This act of confession strips away the layers of self-deception that dull our spiritual ears. Some believers find it helpful to incorporate a daily or weekly practice of examination, asking the Holy Spirit to reveal areas needing repentance. A clean conscience and a contrite spirit are conducive to hearing God clearly.

7.2.2 The Distraction of Worldly Noise

Modern life assaults the senses with incessant noise: constant notifications, media consumption, and overloaded schedules. In such an environment, it becomes challenging to still one's mind and attune to the gentle nudges of the Holy Spirit. Distracted hearts struggle to dwell in reflective prayer, often rushing through quiet times or skipping them altogether. Jesus highlighted the danger of a distracted life in the parable of the sower when He spoke of seeds choked by "the cares of the world and the deceitfulness of riches" (Matthew 13:22).

Overcoming distraction requires deliberate choices. Some believers set boundaries around screen time or designate technology-free zones in the home. Others adopt spiritual rhythms that include daily "quiet hours," journaling, or mindful walks in nature. By reigning in the tyranny of busyness, the believer carves out the mental and emotional space essential for communion with God. Though every personality and season of life is different, the principle remains: hearing God often demands a measure of stillness that modern culture rarely grants freely.

7.2.3 The Weight of Doubt and Unbelief

Just as faith opens the door to God's activity (Matthew 9:29), unbelief can impede it. When believers harbor deep skepticism about whether God speaks personally or whether He would speak to *them*, that disbelief can create a self-fulfilling barrier. James 1:6–8 advises that anyone who asks God for wisdom should do so without doubting, for "the one who doubts is like a wave of the sea." This is not to shame honest questions but to illustrate that persistent cynicism undermines confidence in receiving divine guidance.

A distinction should be made between genuine doubt—where a believer sincerely wrestles with faith questions, seeking resolution—and a hardened unbelief that dismisses God's personal involvement altogether. The former can be a catalyst for deeper understanding, while the latter fosters spiritual deafness. Overcoming ingrained doubt often requires immersing oneself anew in Scripture, remembering God's faithfulness in past experiences, and seeking counsel from mature believers who can address theological or existential concerns. Recounting testimonies—both personal and communal—of answered prayer and divine intervention can also bolster faith that God still speaks.

7.2.4 Emotional Wounds and Fears

Emotional trauma, unresolved grief, or fear can distort one's perception of God and hinder the ability to receive His comfort or direction. For instance, someone who was wounded by harsh, authoritarian figures in early life might subconsciously view God as an overbearing judge, leading them to shrink back from any sense of His voice. Others, plagued by fear of making the "wrong choice," might become paralyzed and unable to discern God's gentle leading.

In such cases, healing is often a process that involves counseling, pastoral care, and personal reflection under the Holy Spirit's guidance. As the soul heals, the individual becomes more receptive to God's voice, no longer filtering His communication through layers of pain or distrust. Passages like Psalm 34:18 ("The Lord is near to the brokenhearted") and Matthew 11:28 ("Come to me, all who labor and are heavy laden, and I will give you rest") remind believers that God's posture is compassionate. As they internalize the truth of His tenderness, they often discover renewed capacity to hear Him speak words of restoration and direction.

7.2.5 The Paralysis of Perfectionism

A less obvious hindrance arises from the fear of error or the desire for flawless certainty. Some believers hesitate to step out in faith regarding a sensed prompting because they worry about getting it wrong. While prudence and testing are vital (as addressed in earlier discussions about discernment), an excessive dread of making mistakes can lead to spiritual stagnation. The narrative of Scripture includes many individuals—Moses, Gideon, Jonah—who initially misunderstood or resisted God's instructions yet eventually fulfilled their callings.

Encountering God's voice is often a learning process. Like a child learning to speak or walk, Christians grow in discernment over time, refining their ability to differentiate divine leading from personal inclination. This journey requires a willingness to act in faith, make course corrections if necessary, and trust that God can redirect a yielded heart. Indeed, a perfectionist mindset that demands 100% clarity before obedience can ironically become a greater obstacle than any honest misstep taken in humility.

7.3 Obedience to the Oracle

Hearing God personally is not an end in itself; rather, it is meant to catalyze transformation. Scripture is replete with narratives demonstrating that divine revelations call for responses—whether repentance, action, worship, or perseverance. The final dimension of receiving God's oracle, therefore, lies in applying it. As Jesus taught in the parable of the wise and foolish builders (Matthew 7:24–27), it is not those who merely hear His words but those who do them who stand firm when storms arise.

7.3.1 The Biblical Imperative of Obedience

In John 14:15, Jesus stated, "If you love me, you will keep my commandments." This linkage between love and obedience underscores a relational dynamic: the believer who truly treasures God's voice responds with submission. Such submission is not legalistic but rooted in trust that God's instructions serve our ultimate good and His larger redemptive purpose. Abraham's prompt obedience in Genesis 12:1–4, leaving his homeland at God's directive, exemplifies how trust in God's character emboldens radical compliance—even when details are unclear.

Obedience also affirms the authenticity of one's faith. James 2:17 declares that faith without works is dead, meaning that a genuine conviction that one has heard God will manifest in tangible decisions or behavior shifts. If a sense of God's prompting to reconcile a broken relationship is repeatedly ignored, for instance, the spiritual ear can grow dull, and the believer may miss further invitations from God.

7.3.2 Practical Steps of Implementation

When receiving a personal directive from God—whether through Scripture, prayer, or a persistent burden—believers often find it helpful to outline specific steps of obedience. For example, if one discerns a call to vocational ministry, the next actions might include prayerfully seeking counsel from church leaders, researching training programs, or volunteering in relevant ministries. Similarly, if a Christian feels convicted about reconciling with a family member, they might begin by drafting a letter or arranging a face-to-face meeting. Breaking obedience into clear, manageable steps reduces overwhelm and translates spiritual conviction into concrete acts.

It is also prudent to integrate wise counsel during this process. Proverbs 15:22 observes that "without counsel plans fail, but with many advisers they succeed." Mature friends, mentors, or pastors can provide perspective, address blind spots, and confirm that the perceived directive aligns with biblical principles. While God sometimes calls individuals to lonely paths of obedience—consider the prophet Jeremiah—He often uses the body of Christ to affirm and support the steps He asks us to take.

7.3.3 The Cost of Obedience

Hearing and obeying God does not guarantee ease or comfort. Indeed, biblical figures who received clear divine mandates often faced challenges, persecutions, or sacrifices. Moses risked Pharaoh's wrath; Daniel confronted threats of death in Babylon; Paul endured shipwrecks, beatings, and imprisonment. While few modern believers face such extreme repercussions, obedience to God's voice can still disrupt personal ambition, require relocation, or test cherished relationships. Yet the cost must be viewed in light of the surpassing worth of God's will.

In Luke 9:23, Jesus called His disciples to "take up their cross daily," suggesting that following Him often involves self-denial. The question is not whether hearing God is advantageous for immediate comfort, but whether we recognize His voice as the supreme authority guiding us to both abundant life and eternal purpose. Over time, many believers discover that obedience, though costly, leads to deeper joy, fulfillment, and testimony of God's faithfulness.

7.3.4 Perseverance and Adaptability

Some instructions from God may involve immediate, one-time actions. Others unfold gradually, requiring ongoing perseverance. Consider Noah, who spent decades building the ark based on God's warning about a coming flood (Genesis 6–8). Such long-term obedience can challenge human patience and expose believers to ridicule or misunderstanding from others. Maintaining momentum often involves revisiting the original conviction, seeking fresh encouragement from Scripture, and recalling past instances of God's guidance.

Additionally, the path of obedience may evolve. Just as Paul's missionary journeys in Acts were occasionally redirected by the Spirit (Acts 16:6–10), believers can find that an initial step of obedience leads to new insights or altered plans. Openness to the Holy Spirit's ongoing direction prevents rigid adherence to a static idea of God's will. Instead, the Christian life becomes a relational adventure, constantly pivoting in response to the One who guides each step.

7.3.5 Fruitful Outcomes of Obedience

When believers respond faithfully to God's personal revelations, they often witness outcomes that confirm His hand at work. These fruits can include:

- **Transformation of Character**: As one consistently aligns with divine guidance, virtues such as love, patience, and humility flourish. Obedience sanctifies the believer, shaping them more closely into the image of Christ (2 Corinthians 3:18).
- **Testimony and Influence**: Obedient believers frequently testify that their courage to follow God's prompting inspires others to trust Him more deeply. In

turn, communities become more robust in faith, seeing that God indeed leads and blesses those who heed His counsel.

- **Greater Sensitivity to God's Voice**: Obedience and spiritual receptivity form a virtuous cycle. Each act of faithful response fine-tunes the inner ear, making future guidance easier to recognize. By contrast, repeated disregard of God's nudges can lead to spiritual dullness.
- **Kingdom Impact**: Whether it is a new ministry birthed, a reconciled relationship, or a deeper prayer movement, obedience often becomes a catalyst for broader kingdom fruit. God's oracles are not arbitrary; they align with His redemptive plan and bring life wherever they are carried out.

In conclusion, this chapter discusses divine communication into the intimate realm of each believer's walk with the Lord. Throughout this chapter, we have seen that while God sometimes speaks in dramatic ways—through visions, angelic visits, or supernatural signs—He more commonly guides His children by the inward witness of the Holy Spirit, the illumination of Scripture, and the counsel of a supportive Christian community. Cultivating a listening spirit involves disciplines of prayer, meditation, fasting, and the intentional pursuit of stillness amidst life's noise.

Yet genuine hearing does not stop at reception; it requires obedience. Through biblical examples and personal testimonies, it becomes evident that when God speaks, He does so with purposeful intent—leading believers to greater freedom from sin, deeper fellowship with Himself, and participation in His kingdom objectives. While barriers such as sin, distraction, doubt, emotional wounds, and perfectionistic fears can impede spiritual hearing, they can be overcome by repentance, deliberate practices of solitude, immersion in scriptural truth, and reliance on the faith community for guidance and correction.

Importantly, hearing God personally is not meant to replace or overshadow the irreplaceable authority of Scripture. Rather, it complements our comprehension of biblical principles with timely, situational insights that help us navigate the complexities of daily life. The same Holy Spirit who inspired the Bible can take its timeless truths and apply them directly to a believer's context—whether guiding career decisions, prompting a change of heart toward a neighbor, or offering solace during trials.

For those longing to experience God's voice more clearly, the path forward includes fostering a heart posture of expectation, stewarding spiritual disciplines, and addressing potential hindrances. As with any skill, growth in spiritual hearing requires perseverance. Failures and misunderstandings may occur along the way, but God's grace is sufficient, and He patiently shepherds His people. Over time, a vibrant relational dynamic emerges: the believer prays, God responds in gentle whispers or providential signals, and each response of obedience leads to deeper intimacy and alignment with His will.

Ultimately, receiving the oracle is about communion—knowing God personally and partnering with Him in His redemptive work in the world. As we become attuned to His voice, we discover not merely a distant divine authority but a loving Father who cares about every facet of our existence. He rejoices in our growth, celebrates our steps of faith, and invites us into ever-expanding levels of spiritual insight and usefulness. Such is the privilege and responsibility of hearing God personally: that we might know Him as He truly is and make Him known in word and deed, to the glory of His name.

Chapter 8: The Judgment Oracle – Warning and Hope

One of the most sobering aspects of biblical revelation is the theme of God's judgment. From Genesis to Revelation, Scripture presents God as both merciful and just—extending grace to sinners while holding them accountable for wrongdoing. Judgment oracles, found throughout the Bible, serve as divine pronouncements that highlight the consequences of persistent disobedience. They function as both warnings, aiming to lead people to repentance, and vehicles of hope, pointing toward renewal and redemption for those who heed God's call.

This dynamic of *judgment and hope* has shaped the theological landscape of Judaism and Christianity alike. In the Old Testament, prophets such as Isaiah, Jeremiah, and Ezekiel delivered scathing indictments against Israel and surrounding nations, yet their messages consistently concluded with visions of restoration. In the New Testament, Jesus Himself issued stern warnings about the fate of unrepentant cities (Matthew 11:20–24) and prophesied the destruction of Jerusalem (Luke 21:20–24). At the same time,

He offered a path of salvation, urging His listeners to believe the good news of the kingdom of God.

Contemplating divine judgment can be unsettling, especially in an age that prefers messages of unqualified acceptance and self-affirmation. Yet ignoring this dimension of Scripture would rob us of a holistic understanding of God's character. The same God who abounds in steadfast love also insists on righteousness and justice. Indeed, the oracles of judgment reveal how deeply God values moral order, how profoundly sin disrupts human flourishing, and how passionately God desires to rescue humanity from the self-destructive path of evil. In the pages that follow, we will delve into examples of judgment oracles in Israel's history, discuss their applicability in the modern world, and conclude by considering the ultimate judgment revealed in the final chapters of Scripture—a judgment that brings renewed creation rather than sheer annihilation.

8.1 Historical Judgment Oracles

Throughout the Old Testament, God repeatedly spoke through prophets to warn individuals, cities, and nations of impending judgment if they persisted in sin. These oracles were not arbitrary outbursts of divine wrath but purposeful revelations intended to confront injustice, idolatry, and covenant unfaithfulness. By examining specific historical cases, we gain insight into how God's warnings combine both retribution for wrongdoing and an invitation to repentance.

8.1.1 Judgment in the Early Narratives

The concept of divine judgment surfaces as early as **Genesis 3**, when Adam and Eve's rebellion in Eden results in humanity's expulsion from the garden. This initial punitive measure underscores a foundational biblical truth: sin carries consequences that fracture humanity's intimacy with God. While not an *oracle* in the technical sense, God's pronouncements to the serpent, the woman, and the man (Genesis 3:14–19) establish the pattern that disobedience yields both judgment and a sliver of future hope—exemplified by the promise that the seed of the woman would ultimately crush the serpent's head (Genesis 3:15).

Later, in **Genesis 6–9**, the story of Noah and the Flood represents a cataclysmic judgment upon widespread human wickedness. "The wickedness of man was great in the earth," we read (Genesis 6:5), prompting God to cleanse creation through the waters of judgment. Yet even amid widespread devastation, God preserves Noah and his family, forging a new beginning. The rainbow covenant in Genesis 9:12–17 epitomizes the divine balance between punishment for sin and the gracious opportunity for re-creation.

8.1.2 Oracles Against Cities: Sodom and Gomorrah, Nineveh, and Others

As biblical history progresses, entire cities come under divine judgment. **Sodom and Gomorrah** (Genesis 18–19) stand as notorious symbols of depravity. God's dialogue with Abraham in Genesis 18 underscores His willingness to spare these cities if even ten righteous individuals could be found. When that threshold is not met, the destruction that follows emphasizes God's intolerance for unchecked wickedness. Nevertheless, the narrative highlights both mercy (rescue for Lot and his family) and justice (the punishment of a city devoted to evil).

The **Book of Jonah** offers a unique perspective on the dynamics of judgment and mercy. Commissioned by God to deliver a warning to the Assyrian capital of **Nineveh**, Jonah initially flees, reluctant to see Israel's enemies spared. Eventually obeying God's command, Jonah proclaims, "Yet forty days, and Nineveh shall be overthrown!" (Jonah 3:4). In a remarkable twist, the inhabitants respond with repentance, prompting God to relent from the threatened calamity. This narrative illustrates that judgment oracles can serve their intended purpose: confrontation leading to genuine transformation. Jonah's personal struggle, however, reveals how divine compassion can clash with human desires for vengeance.

Further examples include oracles against **Babylon, Tyre, and Egypt** as detailed in prophetic books like Isaiah (Isaiah 13–14; 19) and Ezekiel (Ezekiel 26–28; 29–32). These pronouncements condemn arrogance, exploitation, and idolatry in powerful, wealthy nations. While the details differ, a consistent theme emerges: God's sovereignty extends over all lands, not merely Israel. When nations persist in unrighteousness—whether moral corruption, oppression of the vulnerable, or brazen idol worship—divine judgment becomes inevitable. Yet even in these stern messages, glimpses of hope appear, whether in the prophecy of Babylon's eventual downfall leading to Israel's release from exile (Isaiah 14:1–4) or the portrayal of Egypt someday coming to know the Lord (Isaiah 19:21–25).

8.1.3 Judgment Within the Covenant Community: Israel and Judah

The bulk of Old Testament prophetic literature addresses Israel and Judah, God's covenant people. Despite having received the Law at Sinai (Exodus 19–24) and witnessing miraculous deliverances, the nation fell repeatedly into idolatry and injustice. Prophets like **Amos, Hosea, Isaiah, and Jeremiah** condemned social oppression, empty ritualism, and alliances with pagan nations that betrayed trust in Yahweh.

For example, **Amos** indicted the northern kingdom of Israel for exploiting the poor and manipulating scales in the marketplace (Amos 2:6–8; 8:4–6). His oracles also targeted religious hypocrisy, where worship services thrived externally even as the nation's heart grew cold. Ultimately, Israel's persistent rebellion led to the Assyrian conquest of Samaria in 722 BC (2 Kings 17:6–23). Jeremiah, ministering in the southern kingdom of Judah, warned of Babylonian invasion if the people refused to repent of idolatry (Jeremiah 25:8–11). That warning materialized in the exile of 586 BC, when Jerusalem fell and the temple was destroyed (2 Kings 25:8–21).

These histories may seem grim, but they convey a crucial principle: covenant privilege does not exempt one from accountability. If anything, greater knowledge of God amplifies responsibility. Thus, oracles of judgment against Israel and Judah illustrate God's unwavering commitment to holiness and ethical conduct. Simultaneously, the prophets interspersed messages of consolation—assuring a faithful remnant and the eventual restoration of a repentant people. For instance, Isaiah 40–66 envisions a return from exile and a glorious future under God's righteous reign, echoing the consistent biblical motif of hope amid judgment.

8.1.4 The Purpose Behind Judgment Oracles

Why would a loving God issue such severe proclamations? From a theological perspective, these oracles serve multiple functions:

1. **Moral Clarity**: They unveil the gravity of sin. By spotlighting specific evils—violence, injustice, idolatry—divine oracles reinforce moral standards that reflect God's character.
2. **Call to Repentance**: Far from delighting in punishment, God continually extends opportunities for change. Even the threat of destruction can be an act of mercy if it awakens hearts to repentance, as seen in Nineveh's story.
3. **Protection of the Vulnerable**: Many judgments address systemic oppression, defending those on society's margins (widows, orphans, foreigners) who suffer under corrupt regimes (cf. Isaiah 1:16–17).
4. **Upholding Divine Sovereignty**: By demonstrating His governance over nations, God asserts that no empire or people stand beyond His reach. This fosters humility among rulers and citizens alike.
5. **Foreshadowing Greater Redemption**: Prophets often conclude with glimpses of future salvation—a messianic deliverer, a purified remnant, or a new covenant. Judgment is not ultimate; transformation is.

In short, historical judgment oracles reveal a God who is simultaneously righteous and redemptive. While He will not ignore sin, He continually provides a pathway for restoration. Understanding these ancient precedents prepares us for the ongoing relevance of divine warnings in today's world—a topic we explore in the next section.

8.2 Present-Day Relevance of Warnings

Some might argue that the biblical age of judgment oracles is long past, relegated to the era of prophets and ancient monarchies. However, Scripture's testimony suggests that God's moral standards and desire for repentance remain consistent. Indeed, the warnings found in Old Testament narratives and New Testament teachings resonate powerfully in contemporary society, revealing timeless truths about the consequences of collective and individual rebellion.

8.2.1 The Nature of God's Holiness and Human Responsibility

At the heart of all judgment oracles lies the reality that God is holy (Leviticus 19:2). Holiness implies moral perfection—an incompatibility with evil that demands its eradication. Modern culture often downplays absolute morality, yet the biblical portrayal insists that wrongdoing, whether hidden in personal lives or institutionalized in social structures, ultimately faces divine scrutiny. This principle extends beyond Israel's ancient context. When entire societies embrace exploitation, systemic corruption, or moral relativism, the seeds of self-destruction are sown. God's warnings to ancient nations, therefore, become cautionary tales: no collective entity can perpetually flaunt divine laws without repercussions.

On an individual level, Jesus' teachings sharpen the moral demands of the Old Testament, identifying even lustful thoughts or hate-filled words as worthy of judgment (Matthew 5:21–22, 27–28). Contemporary believers who reduce God's commandments to external behaviors miss the broader biblical ethic that addresses the heart's disposition. The relevance of these warnings is clear: each person, standing before a holy God, must grapple with the alignment of their inner life with divine standards.

8.2.2 Social Justice and Modern Implications

Many Old Testament oracles target oppression and social injustice—sins that remain alarmingly prevalent in today's world. Economic exploitation, human trafficking, racial discrimination, and political corruption are just a few contemporary manifestations of what the Bible condemns. Prophets like Amos and Micah would undoubtedly decry the hoarding of wealth by the few at the expense of the many, or the silencing of vulnerable voices. Their calls to "let justice roll down like waters" (Amos 5:24) resonate with movements that seek systemic reform and compassion for marginalized communities.

While modern believers may not label themselves "prophets" in the Old Testament sense, a faithful reading of Scripture compels them to speak against injustice. The biblical tradition of oracles encourages both courage in confronting oppressive structures and humility in recognizing personal complicity. In doing so, the church's role involves not merely pronouncing condemnation but also providing tangible hope—through advocacy, charitable action, and the demonstration of God's reconciling love. Indeed, the same God who brought down tyrannical empires in biblical times can still guide societies toward greater righteousness if people heed His voice.

8.2.3 Personal Warning and the Invitation to Repentance

Divine judgment oracles were never restricted to national sins; they also pierced the conscience of individuals. The transformation of Nineveh began not with a collective policy change but with the king's personal repentance (Jonah 3:6–8). Similarly, modern Christians who sense God's conviction—whether regarding habitual sin, relational bitterness, or ethical lapses—can learn from ancient precedents. The biblical response to an oracle of warning is not self-justification but humility and contrition (1 John 1:9).

Such personal application of judgment themes invites deeper discipleship. The Christian life is not static; it involves ongoing sanctification, whereby the Holy Spirit exposes hidden faults and urges believers to realign with God's holiness. This process requires genuine sorrow over sin, a turning away from destructive patterns, and a renewed commitment to walk in the Spirit's power. In some cases, this might mean restitution to those wronged, the dissolution of unhealthy relationships, or public confession when warranted. While these steps can be painful, they mirror the biblical conviction that genuine repentance precedes restoration.

8.2.4 The Prophetic Role of the Church Today

From a theological perspective, the Church inherits aspects of the prophetic vocation. Though not all believers are called to be prophets, the community as a whole bears witness to God's standards in a fallen world. This witness includes warnings about the spiritual consequences of collective and personal sin, articulated through preaching, pastoral counseling, and various forms of public engagement. By invoking biblical truths, modern Christian leaders can address pressing moral issues, from environmental stewardship to the sanctity of life.

Yet the Church must take heed lest it adopt a posture of self-righteous judgment. Jesus reserved some of His harshest critiques for religious leaders who weaponized moral standards while neglecting compassion (Matthew 23:23–24). If the Church's role is to serve as a channel for God's warnings, it must do so in a spirit of humility, intercession, and love. The objective is never to revel in condemnation but to spur people—both within and outside the Christian community—toward the life-giving grace of the gospel. Such balanced proclamation stands in line with the biblical prophets, who lamented the devastation caused by sin even as they declared its inevitable consequences.

8.2.5 The Pastoral Use of Judgment Passages

In many contemporary Christian settings, sermons on God's judgment are overshadowed by those on love, grace, and blessing. While the latter themes are unquestionably central to the gospel, neglecting judgment passages impoverishes spiritual formation. Pastors and teachers who carefully expound these texts, emphasizing their redemptive aim, can help congregations cultivate a reverent fear of the Lord (Proverbs 9:10), a hatred of injustice, and an awareness of personal accountability.

Practical pastoral approaches might include:

1. **Contextual Teaching**: Explaining the historical and cultural background behind biblical judgment oracles to clarify that they stem from a holy, covenant-keeping God.
2. **Linking Judgment to Hope**: Highlighting that biblical judgment typically includes a vision for renewal, so as not to leave listeners in despair.
3. **Encouraging Communal Repentance**: Occasionally setting aside times in corporate worship for confession of communal sins—materialism, racism, or apathy toward suffering.
4. **Offering Support for Transformation**: Providing resources, small group discussions, or spiritual counseling that guide believers through the often-challenging process of responding to God's conviction.

Such an integrated approach ensures that the Church remains faithful to the full counsel of Scripture, presenting a God who is both just and merciful—a theme ultimately culminating in the final judgment described in the New Testament.

8.3 The Ultimate Judgment and Eternal Word

While God's judgment oracles in the Old Testament and New Testament address specific historical moments, Scripture also points forward to a climactic, universal judgment. This eschatological perspective reframes all earlier examples of divine discipline as previews of a final reckoning. Yet this ultimate judgment, far from being purely catastrophic, carries within it the seed of cosmic renewal—*warning and hope* on a grand scale.

8.3.1 Jesus' Teachings on Final Judgment

Jesus spoke frequently of a future day when all humanity would stand before God's throne. Some of His parables depict a separation of the righteous from the wicked, such as the wheat and tares (Matthew 13:24–30, 36–43) and the sheep and goats (Matthew 25:31–46). These vivid analogies underscore that external religiosity cannot save a person; only genuine alignment with God's will, evidenced by love and obedience, secures eternal fellowship with Him.

In **Matthew 24–25**, often referred to as the Olivet Discourse, Jesus interweaves prophecies about the imminent fall of Jerusalem with allusions to the ultimate end of the age. He urges believers to stay watchful, warning that the day of the Son of Man's return will come unexpectedly (Matthew 24:42–44). This teaching underscores that while God extends grace for repentance, there is a temporal limit: eventual judgment awaits. At the same time, Jesus' parables like the talents (Matthew 25:14–30) encourage stewardship and faithful service, suggesting that readiness for judgment involves active participation in God's kingdom work here and now.

8.3.2 The Book of Revelation's Vision of Judgment and Renewal

No biblical text addresses final judgment more dramatically than **Revelation**. Written by the Apostle John in exile, Revelation portrays a cosmic conflict between God and the forces of evil, culminating in a decisive, triumphant judgment. Chapters 6–19 describe a series of plagues, trumpet blasts, and bowls of wrath that symbolize the dismantling of satanic strongholds and human rebellion. Yet these vivid descriptions are interlaced with calls to repentance (Revelation 9:20–21; 16:9–11), echoing the same pattern seen in the Old Testament: warnings precede destruction so that people might turn to God.

The final chapters (Revelation 20–22) depict the **Great White Throne Judgment** (Revelation 20:11–15) and the unveiling of a **new heaven and new earth** (Revelation 21:1). Here, we find the ultimate oracle of hope: evil is definitively eradicated, tears are wiped away, and God dwells with humanity in perfect fellowship. The "former things" of pain and death pass away (Revelation 21:4), replaced by the eternal, radiant presence of the Lamb. Judgment, therefore, is not an end in itself but the threshold to a renewed cosmos where righteousness reigns. This eschatological vision assures believers that no matter how entrenched evil might appear, it faces inevitable defeat under God's sovereign decree.

8.3.3 The Interplay of Warning and Consolation

Eschatological judgment underscores the seriousness of sin and the holiness of God, but it also testifies to God's redemptive heart. The apostle Peter writes, "The Lord is not slow to fulfill his promise as some count slowness... not wishing that any should perish, but that all should reach repentance" (2 Peter 3:9). This statement summarizes the biblical balance: God's patience delays final judgment to allow maximal opportunity for salvation. When that day arrives, it will indeed be terrifying for those who have spurned His grace, but for those who have responded in faith, it marks the consummation of every promise.

Thus, the final judgment does not stand in contradiction to God's love; it *flows* from it. By eradicating evil and vindicating His people, God reaffirms His covenant faithfulness. Believers who have endured persecution or suffered injustice find in God's judgment the assurance that their cries were heard. Meanwhile, God's willingness to redeem even the hardest of hearts (exemplified by the thief on the cross in Luke 23:39–43) testifies that the door of mercy remains open until the very end. This tension between severe warning and lavish hope shapes the biblical understanding of how final judgment will unfold.

8.3.4 Living in Light of Final Judgment

The New Testament frequently exhorts believers to let the reality of coming judgment shape their day-to-day conduct.

Verses like 2 Peter 3:11–12 ask, "What sort of people ought you to be in lives of holiness and godliness, waiting for and hastening the coming of the day of God?" This rhetorical question links eschatology with ethics. Anticipating God's future evaluation motivates moral vigilance and sacrificial service now.

Practically, this mindset combats complacency. Rather than adopting a fatalistic attitude, Christians who hold to Scripture's portrayal of final judgment see themselves as heralds of grace, calling neighbors and nations to reconciliation with God. Evangelism gains urgency, mission efforts intensify, and personal devotion is enriched by the desire to honor the Lord who will one day set all things right. Far from fueling fanaticism, a proper eschatological outlook cultivates humility—recognizing that none stand righteous apart from Christ's atoning work—and fosters compassion for the lost, since divine wrath is not a trivial matter.

8.3.5 Worship and Reverence in Response to Judgment

Throughout the Bible, divine judgment scenes often segue into worshipful adoration. The Book of Exodus describes the Israelites praising God after the defeat of Pharaoh's army at the Red Sea (Exodus 15:1–21). In Revelation, heavenly hosts break forth in praise as God's just judgments topple Babylon (Revelation 19:1–5). These scenes illustrate that when believers witness or contemplate God's righteous acts, the appropriate response is not hubris but awe-filled worship. Judgment underscores how exalted God truly is, revealing His moral perfection and unwavering commitment to vanquishing evil.

In corporate Christian gatherings, this aspect of worship can be integrated through songs, prayers, or liturgical elements that reference God's justice. Such expressions remind congregants that worship is not confined to celebrating divine blessings but includes honoring God's purity and anticipating the final restoration He has promised. Indeed, acknowledging judgment fosters an environment where grace is prized all the more, for believers recognize the depth of mercy extended to them in Christ. Consequently, the tension between warning and hope evolves into a posture of gratitude—worshipers exult in God's holiness even as they rest in the assurance that He has made them holy by His grace.

In conclusion, this chapter addresses a dimension of biblical revelation that can be unsettling yet is integral to understanding God's character. Far from being a relic of ancient prophetic fury, judgment oracles form part of a redemptive narrative in which God confronts evil and calls people to repentance. These oracles serve essential functions: clarifying moral boundaries, protecting the vulnerable, challenging oppressive powers, and outlining the consequences of impenitence. When societies—past or present—embrace sin on a grand scale, these warning passages flash like a beacon, urging a course correction.

Yet in every biblical instance of judgment, from Noah's ark to the final scenes of Revelation, hope endures. The God who chastises also restores. The orchard that is pruned can yield more abundant fruit. The vision of a new heaven and new earth (Revelation 21–22) gives final shape to this tension, showing that divine wrath and mercy ultimately converge in a world purged of evil and filled with God's radiant presence. Judgment, then, is not the final word; redemption is.

For the modern believer, the lessons of judgment oracles are manifold. First, they encourage humility, underscoring the seriousness of sin and the ongoing need for repentance. Second, they inspire ethical transformation, both individually and societally—reminding us that God's standards of justice remain relevant and that our actions have real consequences. Third, they galvanize mission: if we genuinely believe that a day of reckoning awaits all humanity, then proclaiming the gospel becomes a matter of deep urgency. Finally, they enrich worship, as we contemplate a God who is both fearsomely holy and inexhaustibly loving, worthy of our reverence and our praise.

Thus, as we continue to explore the concept of divine oracles in Scripture, the theme of judgment challenges us to hold reverently the tension between God's righteous indignation and His boundless compassion. Understanding that tension fosters a mature faith—one that neither trivializes sin nor despairs of grace, but instead proclaims with the prophet Isaiah: "Though your sins are like scarlet, they shall be as white as snow" (Isaiah 1:18). In the hands of such a God, judgment is never divorced from mercy, and warning always carries within it the seed of hope.

Chapter 9: The Oracle and the End Times

In the Christian tradition, the topic of the "end times" (or eschatology) stirs a mixture of fascination, trepidation, and hope. From the apocalyptic images in the Book of Revelation to the prophetic discourses of Jesus, Scripture abounds with future-oriented oracles that anticipate the conclusion of this present age. These prophecies are not offered merely to satisfy human curiosity; rather, they serve as a divine roadmap, guiding believers to recognize the outworking of God's redemptive plan and to remain vigilant amid worldly distractions.

The apostolic writers repeatedly emphasize that all of history marches toward a decisive climax—the return of Jesus Christ, the resurrection of the dead, final judgment, and the establishment of a new heaven and a new earth (Revelation 21–22). This ultimate culmination does not emerge haphazardly but follows the designs of a sovereign God who has declared the end from the beginning (Isaiah 46:9–10). End-times prophecies (also called "eschatological oracles") are thus integral to the biblical narrative, enabling the Church to interpret present challenges in the light of future glory.

Throughout this chapter, we will survey key biblical prophecies that await fulfillment, discuss the Church's prophetic calling in tumultuous times, and consider how believers can "live with urgency and faith" without descending into speculative frenzy or neglecting their earthly responsibilities. Ultimately, the biblical vision of the end times is not one of doom but of renewed creation—an invitation for God's people to persevere, proclaim hope, and anticipate the final unveiling of God's kingdom in its fullness.

9.1 Biblical Prophecies Still Awaiting Fulfillment

While much of Old Testament prophecy found realization in the first coming of Christ and in historical events (e.g., the exile, the return from Babylon), the New Testament and certain Old Testament texts also point beyond the Cross and Resurrection to future occurrences. These predictions, sometimes called "unfulfilled prophecies," form the backbone of Christian eschatology. Recognizing their scope and significance helps Christians navigate questions about the world's destiny and their role in it.

9.1.1 Israel and the Nations in Future Perspective

A. Restoration and Renewal of Israel Biblical prophets frequently foresaw a glorious future for Israel, extending beyond the people's return from Babylonian exile. Passages like Ezekiel 36–37 picture a national resurrection—the famous vision of the dry bones, symbolizing Israel's restoration under God's Spirit (Ezekiel 37:1–14). Many interpret these oracles as foreshadowing both the modern regathering of Jewish people to their ancestral land and a broader, ultimate spiritual renewal. Paul's discourse in Romans 9–11 reinforces that God's promises to ethnic Israel remain effectual. Romans 11:26 states, "And in this way all Israel will be saved," sparking debate about how precisely this salvation unfolds. Regardless of interpretive nuances, Scripture indicates that God's covenant with Israel has eschatological dimensions still in process.

B. The Full Inclusion of the Gentiles Complementing the promises about Israel is the Old Testament vision that the nations, too, will come to know Yahweh. Isaiah 2:2–4 pictures a future where people from every nation flock to Zion for instruction in God's ways. The New Testament sees the partial fulfillment of this in the global spread of the gospel (Matthew 28:19–20). Yet Revelation 7:9 portrays a final gathering of "a great multitude that no one could number, from every nation, from all tribes and peoples and languages," worshiping before the throne. Until that ultimate scene is realized, the Church remains engaged in mission, proclaiming Christ among unreached communities.

9.1.2 The Rise of Antichrist and the Final Rebellion

Eschatological literature, especially 2 Thessalonians 2:1–12 and the Book of Revelation, speaks of a future global leader or system often termed the "Antichrist." While speculation abounds about the identity and nature of this figure, Scripture emphasizes a few consistent features:

- **Deception and Apostasy**: The "man of lawlessness" (2 Thessalonians 2:3) will deceive many, leading them away from truth. A great falling away is anticipated, suggesting that even professed believers may be vulnerable to cunning lies if not deeply rooted in God's Word.
- **Opposition to God**: This individual (or empire) exalts itself above all that is called God. In Revelation, the "Beast" wages war against the saints (Revelation 13:7), demonstrating antagonism toward genuine faith.
- **Divine Restraint and Ultimate Defeat**: 2 Thessalonians 2:7 indicates that a restraining power holds back the full revelation of this "man of lawlessness" until God's appointed time. Ultimately, Christ destroys this adversary "with the breath of his

mouth" (2 Thessalonians 2:8). Revelation 19:20 likewise depicts the Beast's downfall at the Second Coming.

Though historically many figures have been labeled "antichrist"—from Roman emperors to political tyrants—Scripture points to a definitive, end-times manifestation of this archetype. Discernment is critical: believers watch for spiritual deception and cling to Jesus' warnings that false messiahs and prophets will proliferate near the end (Matthew 24:24).

9.1.3 The Great Tribulation and Periods of Intense Trial

Jesus, in the Olivet Discourse (Matthew 24–25; Mark 13; Luke 21), foretold a season of unparalleled distress before His return. Terms like "the Great Tribulation" or "Jacob's Trouble" (Jeremiah 30:7) refer to a concentrated era of suffering, persecution, and upheaval. Revelation 6–18 elaborates with symbolic judgments—seals, trumpets, and bowls—indicating cosmic disturbances, ecological catastrophes, and fierce spiritual conflict.

Three broad interpretive stances exist among Christians regarding this tribulation:

1. **Preterist View**: Sees much of this prophecy fulfilled in the first-century destruction of Jerusalem (AD 70), though many preterists still anticipate a future consummation.
2. **Futurist View**: Regards these chapters as largely unfulfilled, pointing to a distinct period prior to Christ's literal, visible return.
3. **Idealist View**: Interprets these passages symbolically, suggesting they depict the ongoing struggle between good and evil throughout church history rather than a one-time event.

Despite these variations, all orthodox perspectives agree that the world experiences great upheaval preceding Christ's final triumph. The tribulation oracles warn believers to remain steadfast in faith, trusting God's sovereign hand even in calamity. The overarching message is that despite turmoil, God's redemptive plan moves inexorably toward restoration.

9.1.4 The Second Coming of Christ

Central to Christian eschatology is the promise that Jesus will return bodily, in power and glory (Acts 1:11; 1 Thessalonians 4:16–17). This event serves as the hinge point of all remaining prophecy—culminating in the defeat of evil, the resurrection of the dead, and the establishment of Christ's millennial kingdom (Revelation 20:1–6, according to some interpretations) or His eternal reign in the new creation (Revelation 21–22).

The New Testament repeatedly exhorts believers to watchfulness, emphasizing that no one knows the exact day or hour of this return (Matthew 24:36). Rather than spur idle speculation, these passages call for moral vigilance, evangelistic urgency, and steadfast hope. Christ's Second Coming is the ultimate "oracle" that awaits fulfillment—an event shaping believers' worldview and daily practice.

9.1.5 The Resurrection and Final Judgment

Though introduced earlier in Scripture (e.g., Daniel 12:2), the full doctrine of a future resurrection is most clearly expounded in the New Testament (1 Corinthians 15). At Christ's return, the dead in Christ rise to immortality, joined by believers who remain alive until that moment (1 Thessalonians 4:13–18). The unrepentant are resurrected for judgment (Revelation 20:11–15), facing a reckoning that Scripture describes in stark terms.

This final judgment not only deals with individuals but also unmasks cosmic powers and principalities. Evil is definitively eradicated, the redeemed enjoy eternal fellowship with God, and the entire creation is liberated from bondage (Romans 8:19–22). Such teaching underscores that Christian hope is not an escapist fantasy but a robust anticipation of divine justice and renewal. For the believer, the resurrection to eternal life is the crowning promise, ensuring that death's sting is vanquished.

9.2 The Role of the Church in Prophetic Times

Given these unfulfilled prophecies, the global Church faces a profound calling to bear witness in a world careening toward eschatological climax. While popular culture often caricatures "end-times believers" as doomsday fanatics, Scripture paints a more nuanced portrait: God's people remain calmly resolute, engaged in mission, and anchored in the eternal Word.

9.2.1 Watchmen on the Wall: Spiritual Discernment

The Old Testament imagery of watchmen (Ezekiel 3:16–21; 33:1–9) resonates powerfully with the Church's vocation today. Watchmen stood on city walls to spot approaching danger or guests; similarly, believers remain spiritually alert to shifts in culture, ideologies, and global events that may signal the intensification of end-times conflict. This watchfulness does not imply sensational date-setting or conspiratorial paranoia; rather, it involves discerning how biblical prophecy informs one's interpretation of significant trends (e.g., moral decline, geopolitical tensions, religious persecutions).

Pastors and Christian leaders often address these issues by guiding congregations to read the "signs of the times" (Matthew 16:3) with wisdom. Yet caution is paramount: erroneous predictions throughout church history remind us to avoid dogmatic pronouncements. Instead, the biblical call is to remain ready, ensuring one's spiritual life is in order and one's moral bearings are rooted in Scripture.

9.2.2 Proclaiming the Gospel to All Nations

Among Jesus' final directives was the Great Commission— "Go therefore and make disciples of all nations" (Matthew 28:19). Many eschatological texts, such as Matthew 24:14, link the global proclamation of the gospel with the culmination of the age: "And this gospel of the kingdom will be proclaimed throughout the whole world… and then the end will come." Consequently, the Church's missionary efforts carry eschatological significance; every tribe, tongue, and nation must hear the good news before history's grand finale.

This impetus drives Christian missions, Bible translation projects, and evangelistic endeavors worldwide. Believers see themselves as participants in a cosmic drama, bridging cultural barriers to ensure that people from remote or unreached regions encounter Christ. Far from an optional program, this mission is intertwined with God's ultimate design for humanity. The end times are not merely about cataclysmic judgments but also about an inclusive invitation: "Whoever desires, let him take the water of life freely" (Revelation 22:17).

9.2.3 Offering Hope in a Chaotic World

End-times prophecy underscores that history may grow darker—morally, politically, and spiritually—before the dawn of Christ's kingdom. In such tumult, the Church can serve as a beacon of hope. Believers hold forth the promise that evil's apparent triumph is transient, that God's justice will prevail, and that tribulation yields to eternal peace. Paul describes believers as "ambassadors for Christ" (2 Corinthians 5:20), charged with reconciling people to God in a time when cynicism and despair threaten to reign.

Local congregations respond by ministering to their communities through acts of compassion and service. Food pantries, medical missions, advocacy for marginalized populations—these actions demonstrate God's love tangibly amid societal upheaval. Social involvement is not divorced from eschatological convictions; rather, it becomes a testimony that Christians, convinced of God's final restoration, labor to reflect His kingdom values now. When people see genuine love and resilience in the face of adversity, they glimpse a foretaste of the world to come.

9.2.4 Intercession and Spiritual Warfare

Biblical eschatology highlights heightened spiritual conflict in the last days (Revelation 12). As the forces of darkness rally for a final assault, the Church is exhorted to "put on the whole armor of God" (Ephesians 6:11) and engage in prayerful warfare. Intercession—a sustained, fervent plea for God's intervention—becomes central. Believers petition for wisdom, protection, revival, and the downfall of demonic strongholds that fuel injustice or persecution.

This intercessory calling resonates with the prophet Daniel, whose prayers coincided with revelations about Israel's future (Daniel 9–10). In the same spirit, modern Christians gather in prayer, contending for breakthroughs in nations hostile to the gospel and for the perseverance of persecuted saints. Far from passivity, such prayer harnesses the reality that ultimate power belongs to God, whose oracles promise that no earthly or spiritual tyranny can withstand His decrees forever.

9.2.5 Avoiding Extremes: Balance in Eschatological Engagement

While the Church embraces its prophetic responsibility, it must resist two opposite errors:

1. **Eschatological Apathy**: Some believers, weary of sensational end-times teachings, ignore the topic entirely. This neglect robs them of biblical warnings and hopes that can fortify faith. Failing to address prophecy can lead to complacency and a truncated worldview lacking eternal perspective.
2. **Obsessive Speculation**: Conversely, some become fixated on every rumor or headline, reading conspiratorial significance into mundane events. This sensational approach often discredits the Christian witness when predictions fail. It can also divert attention from practical discipleship, love for neighbors, and consistent gospel ministry.

A balanced stance regards prophecy as an essential scriptural motif—guiding moral vigilance, spurring evangelism, and nurturing hope—without engendering panic or overconfidence. Christ's own teaching (Matthew 24) weaves watchfulness with humility, acknowledging that certain mysteries remain within the Father's knowledge alone (Acts

1:7). The Church thus stands as a community that proclaims the coming kingdom while being faithful stewards of the present moment.

9.3 Living with Urgency and Faith

Eschatology is not just about future events; it directly shapes how believers conduct themselves today. The hallmark of end-times teaching in the New Testament is a call to personal and corporate holiness, along with robust engagement in God's mission. As the culmination of history draws near, the question becomes: how shall we then live?

9.3.1 A Wake-Up Call to Holiness

Multiple apostolic writings link the anticipation of Christ's return to moral purity. John exhorts, "everyone who thus hopes in him purifies himself as he is pure" (1 John 3:3). Peter challenges believers to be "diligent to be found by him without spot or blemish, and at peace" (2 Peter 3:14). This moral urgency stems from the conviction that at the final judgment, every hidden motive and action will come to light (Romans 2:16). Consequently, living in light of eternity compels the believer to reject hypocrisy, secret sin, and worldly compromise.

This pursuit of holiness does not stem from mere fear of punishment but from love for the One who is returning. Like the parable of the ten virgins (Matthew 25:1–13), the wise remain ready with their lamps lit, signifying hearts aflame with devotion and righteousness. They recognize that the bridegroom's arrival is joyous yet requires active preparation. Hence, end-times awareness calls for introspection: Are we cultivating Christlike character, or drifting into complacent worldliness?

9.3.2 Stewardship of Time and Resources

If history is heading toward a divine climax, how believers use their time, talents, and material resources takes on eternal significance. Jesus' parable of the talents (Matthew 25:14–30) underscores accountability: each servant is entrusted with resources and expected to invest them profitably until the master's return. In eschatological perspective, complacency or laziness wastes precious opportunities to serve God's kingdom.

Modern believers thus consider how their vocations, finances, and leisure pursuits align with God's redemptive mission. Some may be called to foreign missions; others might support evangelistic efforts financially or volunteer in local outreach. Regardless of specific calling, the emphasis is on faithfulness: the God who orchestrates cosmic destiny also commissions each Christian to fulfill unique tasks in the short span of mortal life. Recognizing that "the night is far gone; the day is at hand" (Romans 13:12) spurs zeal to maximize every moment for God's glory.

9.3.3 Encouraging One Another with the Blessed Hope

In times of global instability—wars, economic crises, pandemics—fear can grip hearts. Yet Paul reminds believers to "encourage one another with these words" about the resurrection and Christ's return (1 Thessalonians 4:18). The biblical vision of the future provides an anchor, assuring that no adversity can thwart God's ultimate victory. Churches nurture such encouragement through communal worship, testimonies of God's faithfulness, and preaching that highlights the certain hope of eternal life.

This hope extends to those grieving death, facing chronic illness, or enduring persecution. The promise that "death shall be no more" (Revelation 21:4) and that God "will wipe away every tear" undergirds perseverance. Rather than dismissing present sufferings, eschatological hope contextualizes them: they are birth pangs leading to a new order where righteousness reigns. Believers support one another by sharing this perspective, refusing despair and practicing solidarity in trials.

9.3.4 Practical Readiness and Daily Discipline

The biblical command to "be ready" (Matthew 24:44) calls not for frantic over-preparation but for a steady lifestyle shaped by devotion to Christ. Practical readiness might include:

1. **Persistent Prayer**: Maintaining regular communion with God, interceding for others, and aligning one's desires with God's will.
2. **Scriptural Immersion**: Letting the Word transform values and choices, safeguarding against deception.
3. **Intentional Fellowship**: Commitment to a spiritual community where believers spur each other toward love and good deeds (Hebrews 10:24–25).
4. **Confession and Accountability**: Quickly addressing sin, seeking forgiveness, and mending relationships.
5. **Service and Compassion**: Tangibly demonstrating Christ's love, whether in feeding the hungry or uplifting the marginalized.

These disciplines cultivate a posture of watchful expectancy, not rooted in anxiety but in confident trust that God's timeline will indeed unfold. In a culture intoxicated by instant gratification, the discipline of patient readiness models a countercultural faith.

9.3.5 Proclaiming the Full Gospel—Judgment and Grace

Finally, living with end-times urgency involves faithfully presenting the entire counsel of God. This includes the grace-filled message of redemption through Christ's death and resurrection (Romans 5:8–10) as well as the warning that rejecting this grace invites judgment. A one-sided emphasis on love without referencing sin and accountability distorts the gospel, just as an overemphasis on wrath without hope misrepresents God's character. Balancing these elements echoes the biblical oracles, which consistently weave warning and promise.

Those engaged in evangelism or teaching must resist the temptation to filter out difficult eschatological truths (2 Timothy

4:3–4). While not every conversation necessitates delving into detailed end-times theology, a robust gospel invitation acknowledges that each person faces an eternal decision. Thus, telling others about Christ's imminent return fosters sobriety and an awareness of life's ultimate horizon.

In conclusion, this chapter draws our attention to the grand finale of redemptive history as portrayed in Scripture. Although centuries have elapsed since the New Testament authors penned their prophecies, the Church continues to await the fulfillment of God's final oracles, including the return of Christ, the resurrection of the dead, and the renewal of creation. Far from being abstract doctrines or subjects for speculative debate, these eschatological revelations inform how believers live, pray, and minister in the present age.

In exploring **(9.1) Biblical Prophecies Still Awaiting Fulfillment**, we observed that God's promises to Israel, the rise of Antichrist, the Great Tribulation, the Second Coming, and the final resurrection remain as key pillars of Christian hope. Though interpretations differ regarding the precise timing and sequence of events, the overarching message is uniform: God's sovereign plan marches toward an unassailable victory over evil.

(9.2) The Role of the Church in Prophetic Times emphasizes that believers are not passive observers of this unfolding drama but active participants. As watchmen, the Church discerns the moral and spiritual climate; as evangelists, it proclaims the gospel to every nation; as intercessors, it wages spiritual warfare against oppressive forces; and as a community of hope, it embodies compassion amid turmoil. Balancing vigilance with humility, believers navigate end-times questions without succumbing to sensationalism or apathy.

Finally, **(9.3) Living with Urgency and Faith** underscores that eschatological awareness propels believers toward holiness, stewardship, and mutual encouragement. Rather than inciting escapist behavior, the knowledge of Christ's return impels Christians to love sacrificially, serve diligently, and offer solace to a broken world. Daily disciplines—prayer, Bible study, fellowship, accountability—fortify the Church's readiness. Ultimately, the end times' oracle is not a message of doom but of cosmic renewal, inviting humanity to embrace the fullness of God's redeeming grace.

As this chapter concludes, readers are reminded that the biblical oracles concerning the last days carry both warning and consolation—reflecting the unchanging character of God. Those who stand in awe of His holiness also stand secure in His promise. The final chapter of Scripture (Revelation 22) reiterates that Christ is coming quickly, urging all who hear to respond with a resounding "Amen. Come, Lord Jesus!" In that prayer, believers across generations anchor their faith, ever mindful that the story's end is a glorious new beginning—a consummation where every tear is wiped away and the oracle of God echoes in the everlasting joy of His people.

Chapter 10: Becoming God's Oracle – A Called People

One of the prevailing themes throughout Scripture is that God calls ordinary people to become instruments of His communication—His "oracles"—in a broken world. While the Bible speaks of singular prophets who delivered urgent messages, it also envisions an entire community imbued with God's Spirit, empowered to bear witness to divine truth and grace. The New Testament describes believers collectively as a "royal priesthood" (1 Peter 2:9), echoing Old Testament language that frames God's people as mediators of His presence among the nations (Exodus 19:5–6).

The transition from seeing ourselves solely as recipients of God's Word to participants in His ongoing revelation marks a significant shift. We move from reading or hearing the oracle to **becoming** the oracle—walking testaments to divine love and holiness. Yet this role is neither self-appointed nor casual. It arises from God's sovereign calling and demands spiritual formation that refines our character, informs our words, and shapes our actions in ways that reflect God's heart.

The goal of this final chapter is to illuminate how a community of ordinary believers can faithfully embody this calling, becoming God's mouthpiece of comfort, conviction, hope, and clarity to a world often mired in confusion. It emphasizes the interplay between speech and lifestyle, reminding us that one cannot effectively speak God's truth if one's life contradicts that very message. In doing so, it draws upon biblical precedents, pastoral wisdom, and examples of individuals who, throughout church history, have embraced this vocation with transformative impact.

10.1 Speaking God's Truth with Love

In an age saturated with words—spoken and written—the believer who speaks on God's behalf has a solemn responsibility to ensure that speech aligns with divine truth and reflects divine love. The epistle of James cautions, "Not many of you should become teachers... for you know that we who teach will be judged with greater strictness" (James 3:1). While this warning applies specifically to those in teaching roles, the principle stands for all who carry the message of the gospel: words are powerful, and misusing them can cause harm. On the other hand, speaking truth in a spirit of love can bring transformation, encouragement, and clarity.

10.1.1 The Biblical Basis for a Speaking People

Scripture repeatedly showcases God's delight in using human voices to accomplish His redemptive purposes. From Moses confronting Pharaoh (Exodus 5) to Esther pleading before the king for her people (Esther 7), God often delegates the task of speaking to those willing to stand in the gap. In the New Testament, Jesus commissions His disciples, saying, "You will be my witnesses" (Acts 1:8). He promises the Spirit's empowerment so they can testify of His resurrection, salvation, and lordship. This reveals that the church is not to remain silent. Rather, believers are authorized—and indeed commanded—to proclaim God's truth (Matthew 28:19–20).

Beyond formal preaching or teaching, every believer can bear God's Word in daily contexts: workplaces, families, social circles. Colossians 4:6 advises, "Let your speech always be gracious, seasoned with salt," implying that conversations themselves can become holy ground where God's perspective is gently and respectfully introduced. In this way, "speaking God's truth" transcends pulpits and seminaries; it permeates the everyday rhythms of life.

10.1.2 Overcoming Fear and Timidity

Despite biblical mandates, fear often hinders believers from speaking up. Fear of rejection, ridicule, or failure can silence God's people. Timothy, a young church leader, wrestled with timidity, prompting Paul to remind him: "God gave us a spirit not of fear but of power and love and self-control" (2 Timothy 1:7). This exhortation resonates today. Believers must confront the inner voices that question, "Am I qualified? Will I be misunderstood?" and respond with faith that God equips those He calls.

Prayer is pivotal in this battle. The early Christians, upon facing threats, prayed for boldness, and "they were all filled with the Holy Spirit and continued to speak the word of God with boldness" (Acts 4:31). Fear dissipates when anchored in the awareness that the same Spirit who anointed prophets and apostles indwells modern believers, enabling them to speak precisely what is needed in each situation (Luke 12:12).

10.1.3 The Synergy of Truth and Love

Ephesians 4:15 instructs believers to be "speaking the truth in love." This dual emphasis guards against two extremes: unloving truth-telling and love devoid of truth. Truth absent love can become harsh dogmatism, wounding rather than healing. Love absent truth can deteriorate into passive affirmation that tolerates destructive behaviors. In God's economy, truth is never meant to be a bludgeon; it is a beacon guiding people toward redemption. Simultaneously, love is never an excuse to ignore wrongdoing or deny difficult realities.

Cultivating this synergy demands wisdom. The Holy Spirit enables believers to discern the right moment, tone, and approach for each situation. For instance, Jesus, whose ministry perfectly embodied this principle, spoke gentle words to the penitent but firm rebukes to the self-righteous (Matthew 23). Whether confronted with a friend's moral compromise or a cultural debate about ethics, the believer who has internalized God's character can offer an oracle that marries clarity with compassion.

10.1.4 Real-Life Contexts: Evangelism, Apologetics, Advocacy

A. Evangelism: Sharing the gospel with a seeker or skeptic necessitates both factual clarity—explaining who Jesus is and why His sacrifice matters—and relational sensitivity. The aim is not to win an argument but to invite a person into reconciled relationship with God (2 Corinthians 5:18–20).

B. Apologetics: When defending the Christian worldview, believers may address philosophical challenges or moral controversies. This environment requires a gentle, respectful posture (1 Peter 3:15). By weaving personal testimony with scriptural wisdom, the Christian communicator becomes a living oracle, testifying that God's truth is not abstract dogma but a reality shaping one's entire being.

C. Advocacy for the Marginalized: Sometimes speaking God's truth means giving voice to the voiceless, denouncing injustice, or highlighting systemic sins that oppress communities. In line with biblical prophets who championed the poor (Amos 5:24), modern believers can become conduits of divine concern for issues such as trafficking, poverty, or racism. Such actions require moral courage, stepping beyond comfort zones to confront societal powers.

In each scenario, the believer's motivation must be love for God and for neighbor (Matthew 22:37–39). Where that love is genuine, the words spoken become channels of grace, conviction, and hope.

10.2 Living a Prophetic Lifestyle

While words matter greatly, a person's life can sometimes speak more eloquently than any sermon. It is incongruous for a believer to proclaim divine truths while living in a manner that contradicts them. As the apostle John writes, "Let us not love in word or talk but in deed and in truth" (1 John 3:18). Embracing a "prophetic lifestyle" means embodying the values, holiness, and compassion that reflect God's character. In doing so, we become a tangible oracle—our actions testifying to God's reality in the present.

10.2.1 The Meaning of a Prophetic Lifestyle

Often, the term "prophetic" is conflated with foretelling future events or delivering ecstatic utterances. Yet a more holistic view includes **forthtelling**—demonstrating and declaring God's perspective in current realities. A prophetic lifestyle, then, is one that visibly challenges prevailing cultural norms by embodying Kingdom ethics: honesty in business, humility in leadership, selflessness in relationships, and justice in social structures. It resonates with Jesus' prayer: "Your kingdom come, your will be done on earth as it is in heaven" (Matthew 6:10).

Such a life challenges complacency, calling people to see that God's ways are indeed higher than human ways (Isaiah 55:9). It also fosters curiosity. When neighbors observe a family fostering children in need or a business leader forgoing unethical profit for the sake of integrity, they witness a living sermon. These choices communicate something transcendent. In this sense, every Christian can be a "prophetic signpost," directing onlookers to consider the God who inspires such radical love and fidelity.

10.2.2 Holiness, Integrity, and Alignment with God's Heart

At the core of a prophetic lifestyle lies **holiness**—not the superficial moralism of legalistic rules, but a genuine separation from sin and devotion to God. The apostle Peter echoes Leviticus 11:44 when he writes, "Be holy, for I am holy" (1 Peter 1:15–16). This call to holiness is not about self-righteous isolation but about reflecting the divine nature in character and deed. In a culture that often normalizes dishonesty, sensual indulgence, or narcissism, a believer who consistently practices purity stands out like a beacon.

Integrity is another linchpin. Consistency between proclaimed beliefs and daily actions cements one's credibility as God's oracle. Jesus castigated hypocrisy in the Pharisees, labeling them "whitewashed tombs" (Matthew 23:27). When individuals espouse biblical principles yet exploit others in business or relationships, they undermine the gospel message. Conversely, a life of integrity—faithful to one's promises, kind under stress, generous with resources—reinforces the authenticity of one's testimony.

Ultimately, these outward virtues flow from **alignment with God's heart**. Believers who spend time in Scripture and prayer develop sensitivities to what grieves or pleases God. Their priorities shift toward eternal values, fueling a sacrificial love for others that cannot be manufactured through mere religious duty. Indeed, the Holy Spirit becomes the internal sculptor, molding disciples into Christ's likeness so they can effectively convey His message (2 Corinthians 3:18).

10.2.3 Social Justice and Caring for the Marginalized

A prophetic lifestyle inevitably includes a concern for the vulnerable and oppressed, echoing the biblical prophets who denounced exploitation and championed the cause of the widow, orphan, and foreigner (Isaiah 1:17; Zechariah 7:10). Jesus' parable of the Good Samaritan (Luke 10:25–37) underscores that genuine faith cannot ignore neighbors in need. Accordingly, believers who feed the hungry, care for refugees, or advocate for equitable laws embody the compassion of a God who hears the cry of the afflicted (Psalm 10:17).

This commitment transcends political affiliations or social programs—it is rooted in the conviction that each person bears God's image (Genesis 1:27). When a local church runs a homeless shelter or invests in community development, it performs more than mere charity; it testifies to a higher Kingdom ethic. In doing so, these actions prophesy a future where righteousness dwells (2 Peter 3:13). They also validate the spoken gospel, showing skeptics that Christian faith is not just an abstract creed but a force for tangible transformation.

10.2.4 The Role of the Holy Spirit in Daily Guidance

While abiding principles like love, holiness, and integrity guide a prophetic lifestyle, believers also need moment-by-moment discernment. The Holy Spirit, promised by Jesus as the Comforter and Guide (John 16:13), provides this. Walking "in the Spirit" (Galatians 5:16) involves a posture of attentive listening, where believers remain open to spontaneous nudges—perhaps to pray for a colleague, share an encouraging word, or hold back a harsh retort.

Such Spirit-led spontaneity can lead to surprising encounters. One might sense a prompting to befriend a lonely neighbor, only to discover they had been praying for companionship. Alternatively, a believer might feel burdened to intercede for someone's healing or deliverance and witness a breakthrough that glorifies God. Though the specifics differ, the principle remains: the Holy Spirit empowers ordinary Christians to enact God's love in real-time, extending the possibility of encountering God through daily interactions. This lifestyle is "prophetic" in that it reveals God's heart and intentions to the world around us.

10.2.5 Avoiding Pitfalls: Pride, Self-Righteousness, and Burnout

Walking a prophetic path comes with risks. Chief among them is **pride**—the temptation to view oneself as more enlightened or "spiritual" than others. Jesus faced this issue with some Pharisees who prided themselves on piety but lacked compassion (Mark 7:6–8). Today, believers who adopt a judgmental attitude or flaunt their moral achievements undermine God's message. Scripture insists that God "resists the proud, but gives grace to the humble" (James 4:6). A truly prophetic individual maintains humility, attributing all virtue and insight to divine grace.

Self-righteousness is a related danger. When moral convictions morph into legalistic condemnation of others, the gospel's central note of redemption can be lost. While believers must stand for truth, they do so as recipients of mercy, not as faultless critics. Recognizing one's own ongoing need for grace fosters empathy, enabling a prophetic voice that challenges wrongdoing while still valuing the person in error.

Lastly, **burnout** can afflict those passionately devoted to God's cause. The prophet Elijah, after intense spiritual victories, fell into despair (1 Kings 19:4). In modern contexts, activism, ministry, and crisis intervention can deplete emotional and physical reserves. A sustainable prophetic lifestyle requires rhythms of rest, sabbath, and spiritual replenishment—practices that preserve joy, resilience, and the capacity to continue serving effectively.

10.3 Leaving a Legacy of Truth

Becoming God's oracle is not a mere one-generation endeavor; it spans the centuries, as each group of believers imparts divine wisdom to the next. The baton of truth must be carefully handed over, ensuring that future generations remain anchored in Scripture and bold in proclaiming God's message. While the impetus often lies on older believers, younger believers likewise share responsibility for receiving, stewarding, and extending that legacy.

10.3.1 Mentoring the Next Generation

The apostle Paul modeled spiritual mentorship when he took Timothy under his wing (Philippians 2:19–22; 1 Timothy 1:2). Timothy, in turn, would become a faithful pastor, further propagating the gospel legacy. This pattern affirms a biblical principle: truth is best transmitted in relational contexts where teaching, encouragement, and correction flow naturally.

Local churches can foster mentorship through formal programs—pairing seasoned believers with new converts or youth—or through informal gatherings, small groups, or workshops. In such spaces, the older generation shares life lessons, scriptural insights, and testimonies of God's faithfulness, encouraging the younger to adopt a similar zeal for God's oracle. Mentors also teach spiritual disciplines, critical thinking, and moral discernment, equipping the next wave of believers to stand firm amid cultural shifts.

10.3.2 The Church as a Multi-Generational Entity

Biblically, the people of God have always included diverse age groups, from children to elders (Joel 2:28). Each cohort brings unique perspectives and gifts. Yet in some modern contexts, generational gaps can hinder unity—traditional worship preferences might clash with contemporary expressions, or older believers might feel disconnected from digital-savvy youth. Overcoming these divides is crucial to maintaining a cohesive witness.

When congregations intentionally create intergenerational fellowship—through service projects, prayer gatherings, or shared mission trips—they cultivate deeper empathy and learning. Younger believers can glean wisdom from the life experiences of seniors, while older believers gain renewed energy and fresh approaches to outreach. This synergy reflects Paul's metaphor of the church as a body (1 Corinthians 12:12–27), where each part contributes something indispensable. Indeed, a vibrant multi-generational church becomes an oracle of hope in a fragmented society, demonstrating that unity in Christ transcends age barriers.

10.3.3 Innovation and Tradition in Delivering God's Message

Every generation faces new cultural dynamics, communication channels, and moral dilemmas. While the substance of God's message remains unchanging—centering on Christ's redeeming work, God's holiness, and human responsibility—methods of delivery often evolve. The early church employed hand-copied manuscripts and public forums. Later eras embraced the printing press, radio, and television. Today, believers leverage social media, podcasts, and other digital platforms.

Striking a balance between **innovation and tradition** is vital. Tradition grounds the church in orthodoxy, safeguarding against doctrinal drift. Innovation ensures the gospel engages contemporary minds and hearts. For example, a church might maintain liturgical elements that anchor it in historic faith while simultaneously producing creative online content that reaches younger or global audiences. Such adaptability expands the oracle's reach, preventing the church from becoming insular or outdated.

Within this context, mentors can encourage younger believers to harness their technological fluency for God's glory, while younger generations can appreciate the rich theological depth and historical perspective that older believers bring. The objective is not to idolize novelty but to steward each era's communication tools so that the gospel resonates powerfully without diluting its core.

10.3.4 Overcoming Generational and Cultural Divides

Besides age, cultural differences—ethnic, linguistic, socioeconomic—pose challenges for a unified gospel witness. In the first-century church, Jewish and Gentile believers wrestled with divergent customs, yet Paul insisted on unity in Christ (Ephesians 2:11–22). Modern congregations replicate this tension. The complexity of language barriers, economic disparities, and cultural worldviews can lead to misunderstandings or even partial segregation. If the church is to remain a compelling oracle, it must embody the reconciling power of the gospel across these divides.

Practical steps might include:

1. **Multilingual Services or Gatherings**: Reflecting the diversity of a region by providing translation or bilingual worship to ensure everyone feels included.
2. **Shared Leadership**: Inviting leaders from different cultural backgrounds to share teaching responsibilities or collaborate in decision-making.
3. **Cross-Cultural Training**: Organizing workshops that educate congregants about various traditions, bridging gaps that could lead to prejudice.
4. **Joint Outreach**: Partnering across congregations with distinct cultural identities to serve the broader community, modeling unity to a fragmented society.

Such efforts reflect God's ultimate design for a people "from every tribe and language and people and nation" (Revelation 5:9), collectively proclaiming His praises. By overcoming segmentation, the church testifies to a reconciled humanity under Jesus' lordship, thereby reinforcing its credibility as God's oracle.

10.3.5 The Harvest is Plentiful, the Laborers are Few

While efforts to pass on truth may seem daunting, Jesus' assurance remains: "The harvest is plentiful, but the laborers are few" (Luke 10:2). History testifies that whenever believers commit to faithful living and proclaim God's Word with authenticity, fruitfulness follows. This assurance invites believers to prayerful expectation. The Holy Spirit continues drawing hearts to Christ, and God's Word does not return void (Isaiah 55:11).

Consequently, leaving a legacy of truth involves more than preserving doctrinal statements—it means igniting a passion for evangelism, discipleship, and social renewal in the next generation. As younger believers catch this vision, they become the new wave of God's oracles, fully equipped for challenges and opportunities unique to their cultural moment. They carry forward the unchanging gospel in ways that resonate with emerging contexts, ensuring that the church's witness remains robust and relevant.

In conclusion, this chapter encapsulates a profound yet deeply practical reality: the God who once spoke through prophets, apostles, and Scripture still speaks today through a worldwide community of believers. While the preceding chapters highlighted the nature of divine revelation in biblical times and the ways God continues to reveal Himself, this final chapter underscores the believer's active participation in that legacy. We are not mere listeners; we are also commissioned communicators.

The chapter's three focal points illuminate how this calling unfolds:

1. **Speaking God's Truth with Love**: Through prayerful dependence on the Holy Spirit, believers overcome fear to become voices of clarity and compassion. Truth, tempered by humility, unlocks hearts rather than closing them. Whether sharing the gospel in personal conversations or addressing wider cultural issues, Christians can become conduits of hope, addressing real human needs with both conviction and empathy.
2. **Living a Prophetic Lifestyle**: Beyond words, the church's moral integrity and sacrificial actions constitute a living sermon. Each believer's consistent embodiment of holiness, justice, and compassion underscores the authenticity of the message. By resisting sin, championing the marginalized, and operating under the Spirit's guidance, Christians demonstrate the practicality of divine wisdom in everyday life.
3. **Leaving a Legacy of Truth**: True transformation is sustained when older believers disciple the young, communities bridge generational and cultural gaps, and innovative expressions of faith honor time-tested doctrine. This multi-generational handoff ensures the gospel endures despite shifting societal landscapes. Each generation stands on the shoulders of those before it, inheriting a commission to serve as God's oracle in new contexts.

In the end, the church's role as "God's oracle" centers on reflecting Christ—His character, His teachings, His redemptive power—to a world in desperate need of divine perspective. This vocation is not restricted to clergy or professional ministers; it extends to every believer willing to let God shape their speech and lifestyle. The echoing refrain of 2 Corinthians 5:20 rings true: "We are ambassadors for Christ, God making his appeal through us." Such is the privilege and responsibility of a called people.

Thus, this chapter—and indeed the entire book—closes with an invitation for every reader to embrace this identity. May you hear God's voice calling, "Whom shall I send?" (Isaiah 6:8), and may you respond, "Here am I! Send me." As you do, you step into the lineage of faithful men and women who have carried the divine oracle across centuries, speaking life into dead places, shining light in darkness, and steadfastly pointing all who listen to the One who reigns forever in truth and love.